*Toward
a Christian
Political Ethics*

JOSÉ MÍGUEZ BONINO

Toward
a Christian
Political Ethics

FORTRESS PRESS   Philadelphia

Library of Congress Cataloging in Publication Data

Míguez Bonino, José.
  Toward a Christian political ethics.

  1. Christian ethics. 2. Sociology, Christian.
3. Christianity and politics. 4. Liberation theology.
I. Title.
BJ1251.M53 1983   241'.62   82–48541
ISBN 0–8006–1697–9 (pbk.)

9765A83   Printed in the United States of America   1–1697

Contents

Preface

These men and women, these groups, have to "process," they have to "put in black and white" the experience of these last decades, a passionate and terrible experience—paid many times in blood—of an intensity and complexity that certainly has had no parallel in the Christian history of our continent.

The above passage came to me anonymously, without date or place of origin, like so many similar writings in Latin America today. It came in the mail as part of a five-page paper entitled "Christian Commitment and Politics." The paper represents an attempt to evaluate more than fifteen years of active participation on the part of many Christians in the political struggle for liberation. As one reads these simple lines—in which one can hear the echo of personal experiences, of long talks with friends, of consultations in small groups meeting here and there, of provisional drafts of essays written for internal use—two aspects of the common experience appear in bold relief. It is my hope that this book will bear witness to both of them.

In the first place, Christians active in political life have experienced the condition of being "thrown" into a world for which they were not prepared. "They have had to learn how crudely ambiguous and dirty political life is." There is the initial enthusiasm of having "finally" found a form of action that could help make their Christian concern for life and justice come true, but then that enthusiasm comes smack up against all "the disappointments that await those who engage in that kind of undertaking." But there is also an awareness of their inability as Christians to understand and to account to themselves for the meaning of what they are doing: "Coming from a confessional world that possesses its own language and mystique, they were forced to enter a different world having radically different ideas, language, and rules of the game." The political experience has been a school of humility, teaching Christians to be humble—humble about themselves and the claims of their faith, and humble also about the possibilities and claims of politics.

But strangely enough, "in the midst of so many questions" some "certainties" have emerged as well: "Ignored and even rejected by their churches ... disconnected or isolated ... a deep and warm tie with 'Christian reality' remains alive in them." And there emerges in them the conviction "in spite of everything and against everything to remain faithful to the human commitment and faithful to God." Theirs is the conviction that we must "courageously resume our position as believers and dare to 'name God,' to confess him from within the womb of politics, from within the very heart of commitment." To "name God" means to "denounce and condemn all the new idolatries, all claims of the ideologies and systems to being perfect and absolute." But it also means to "stake one's life with and for the poor—not only those poor who have no bread, for whom all the revolutions of the world are undertaken, but also all the poor of humankind, those of unimpressive proportions, those who are different from the majority, those whom the revolutionary movements tend to undervalue and even annihilate."

I have quoted at length from this simple but honest document because it bears witness to a fact that Christians throughout the world can no longer evade: if we intend to live our faith as a reality in today's world, we cannot avoid coming to grips with this "thing" that shapes individual and collective life, that both confers meaning on and denies meaning to human plans and actions, that encompasses and invades all areas of human existence, and that offers and dispenses both life and death to thousands of millions—political struggle! When Christians do come to grips with politics, however, it becomes necessary for our faith to die and be resurrected. We have to learn anew to name God and confess Christ, to believe and to be church, to pray and receive the sacrament, to be "holy" and to expectantly wait for "life eternal." This small book is meant, in the first place, simply to witness to this fact— not to give answers but to witness!

But this book intends also to be an acknowledgment of the long and sustained effort on the part of many Christians throughout the world to think through their Christian responsibility for the world and to offer to the churches their joint reflection and some tools to assist them in meeting their responsibilities in this area. I refer to the ecumenical work of the last fifty-five years. From the invitation to join hands across confessional lines in order to rebuild Europe after the First World War (Stockholm 1925), through the struggle to witness to Christ's sovereignty in face of the claims of totalitarianism (Oxford 1937) and the search for a "responsible society" (Amsterdam 1948), to the confrontation with the "technological and political revolutions" of our time (Geneva 1966), the ecumenical movement has accumulated a treasure of experience which in recent years has posed certain critical demands. There is first the demand to shape a vision that can mobilize Christians to seek a new society, a vision in which hope for the kingdom that God alone can bring will act not as a deterrent but as a spur to human responsibility in the world. But at the same time there is the demand for understanding, for a consistent and realistic articulation of the Christian's way of facing the dilemmas and ambiguities of political life. The call to develop a "Christian political ethics" and to give shape to the vision of "a just, participatory, and sustainable society" has emerged as the concrete program of the World Council of Churches in this area of the churches' witness.

These then are the two worlds of experience and challenge to which I hope this book can make a contribution—Christians committed to the struggle for liberation, and the concerns of the ecumenical movement in the area of political ethics. The contribution I intend is modest: to clarify as much as I can the nature of the question, to illustrate it from past and present experience in Latin America, and to add a few "theological footnotes." The book can perhaps serve as an invitation to Christian political ethics. If others—whether sympathetic to my approach or irritated by it—are moved to carry through the task with greater experience, knowledge, and depth, my audacity in publishing these pages will have been justified.

This book moves, however inadequately, in the realm of "theory." Many friends who have staked their lives in the struggle will be impatient with it. I understand and share this impatience. But I am also convinced that we underestimate the theoretical task and turn our backs on theory only at a considerable cost to ourselves and to the effectiveness of our own action. The cost in human life and suffering that we pay for simple pragmatism is too high. Theory is necessary, in the first place, because it is unavoidable; whether acknowledged or not, it is present. It is necessary in order that we can make explicit to ourselves the presuppositions and assumptions of our action as well as expose and critically examine forms of action suggested to us. It is necessary also in order to give unity and coherence to the struggle. Finally, it is necessary in order that we can make available our experience and transmit it to others, inviting them to join the effort. But we must also acknowledge that theologians are singularly ill-prepared for a theoretical work that must necessarily be interdisciplinary in nature, dealing as it does with an area (political life) and a group of sciences (the social sciences in general) with which they have usually had little experience. Nevertheless the work has to be undertaken. I have therefore decided to risk publishing these chapters, knowing that competent theologians and competent social scientists both will probably find in them serious mistakes and shortcomings.

The list of people to whom I would express my gratitude is too long to enumerate. It includes the professors and students at Union Theological Seminary in Richmond, Virginia, where the substance of the book was originally delivered as the Sprunt Lectures; Columbia Theological Seminary in Decatur, Georgia, where I delivered the Smyth Lectures; and Perkins School of Theology in Dallas, Texas, where I delivered the Fondren Lectures—to all of them I am deeply grateful for the generous invitation, the stimulus, and the fruitful interchange. The list also includes students from several other seminaries and schools of theology, colleagues in teaching and in the ecumenical movement, friends, and above all the many—well-known and unknown—persons who, among and beyond the groups I have mentioned, have opted to make "deliverance of the captives" their life-response to the free grace of Jesus Christ. I am only trying to return to them—as it has been reflected in my own consciousness and thinking—what they have given me, in the hope that in the Power and Love that exceeds ours it may be of some use.

Buenos Aires   José Míguez Bonino
February 8, 1983

1

The Need
for a Political Ethics

For a long time theology claimed to be the queen of sciences. But long before the era of Christian theology, one of the most influential thinkers in the history of humankind had seen things rather differently. Speaking of "the chief good," Aristotle said that we must try to "determine what it is, and of which of the sciences or capacities it is the object. It would seem to belong to the most authoritative art and that which is most truly the master art. And *politics* appears to be of this nature; for it is this that ordains which of the sciences should be studied in a state, and which each class of citizens should learn and up to what point they should learn them."[1] Whatever the intrinsic intellectual merits of his viewpoint, we must agree that Aristotle at least *sounds* much closer to our contemporary experience than do his scholastic disciples. For it does indeed seem increasingly true that "politics uses the rest of the sciences"; it subordinates everything to its "end," as the Stagirite claims.

THE OMNIPRESENCE OF POLITICS

If for the moment we take "politics" in the most elemental meaning of the term, as the sum total of all the relations that go to make up life in a particular society, we can easily see that all the marked tendencies in modern life—urbanization, science-technology, bureaucratization, communications—tend to "politicize" our life, that is, to make of every act a social or public act in which not only primary—face-to-face—relations but also complex secondary relations are involved.

Some seventy-five years ago Edward Ross, a man of the Social Gospel age, already made the point quite graphically:

Nowadays the water main is my well, the trolley car my carriage, the banker's safe my old stocking, the policeman's billy my fist. My own eyes and nose and judgment defer to the inspector of food, or drugs, or gas, or factories, or tenements, or insurance companies. I rely upon others to look after my drains, invest my savings, nurse my sick, and teach my children. I let the meat trust butcher my pig, the oil trust mold my candles, the sugar

11

trust boil my syrup, the coal trust chop my wood, and the barbed wire company split my rails.[2]

Whether we like it or not, in such a situation two things become crystal clear. On the one hand, we can no longer ignore this complication, that all our acts have become collective acts and—to the extent that we are aware of this fact—that we are also responsible. On the other hand, we cannot exercise this responsibility in an individualistic and isolated way but only collectively through structures of responsible participation. In other words, problems of personal ethics have become questions of social ethics.

It seems that two basic factors that are widely recognized as characteristic of the modern world are pulling us in opposite directions. Modern men and women, we are told, understand themselves as "subjects," as the active protagonists of history. They claim control of their world, their life, their destiny. They are no longer content to be the passive "objects" of external powers whether celestial or terrestrial. They are "autonomous" subjects, people "come of age," of whom we have heard so much. But at the same time, in the complex nexus of relations that the modern economy weaves around the world, decisions and actions taken in distant places are incorporated into a total system that in decisive ways affects my individual life. And conversely, my decisions and actions similarly have consequences for millions of other people throughout the world who either suffer or rejoice as a result of what I do:

> The crops in Argentina, the American embargo of wheat to the USSR, the European Common Market, the crop surplus in France, and hunger in India are all part of the same web. A transistor radio made in Korea, which I buy here at a low price, involves the low salary of the workers, the repressive regime in Korea, Japanese economic policies, American capital (which may even include investment funds of the churches), unemployment in my own country, and problems which will involve my children and grandchildren.[3]

In short, all decisions become political decisions. Commenting on the problems of the automobile industry, columnist Richard Reeves concludes: "The choice between a Ford Escort and a Toyota Corolla is a political choice."[4]

SCIENCE-TECHNOLOGY AND THE MULTINATIONALS—TWO TYPICAL EXAMPLES

We can now advance a step further in our analysis of this "omnipresence of politics." We do so by making brief reference to two interrelated examples—the problem of science-technology and the occupation of the economic space in our modern world by the transnationals.

According to historians of science, two facts characterize the development of the last thirty or forty years. On the one hand, the distinctions between basic and applied science and between science and technology have tended to become more or less blurred; we are now faced with a single scientific-technological complex that penetrates every area of life—to such an extent that the environment for human life is no longer "nature" but "techno-nature." On the other hand, this powerful complex is totally dependent on plans, goals, and resources that are determined by decisions made at a different level—economic, political, in many instances even military. As a result, science-technology has become decisively political because: (1) as never before, science is power; (2) the direction in which science develops has a determining effect on all of life—a "science policy" is in fact one of the crucial factors in any reflection on the future of humankind; and (3) the mechanisms for determining and controlling this direction are in the hands of groups or organizations which themselves need to be brought to some form of accountability to the human community.

But can this be done? Not long ago a scientist expressed his opinion:

Political norms and goals are replaced by the objective exigencies of scientific-technical civilization, which are not posited as political decisions and cannot be understood as norms of conviction or Weltanschauung. Hence, the idea of democracy loses its classical substance, so to speak. In place of the political will of the people there emerges an objective exigency, which man himself produces as science and labor.[5]

This would be Aristotle in reverse! Here political ethics vanishes; human decision becomes only an inference, and technological reason takes over—we need only submit to its "objective exigencies."

The hoax, of course, is not difficult to identify: the "objective exigencies" are themselves the result of previous human decisions involving vested interests and ideological or Weltanschauung convictions. No other proof of this is needed than the statistics about the relationship between science-technology and the military-industrial complex. The fact is that politics does *not* disappear; it simply goes underground.

This brief discussion of the power of science-technology leads almost inevitably to a consideration of that other massive development of our time, the transnational corporation. The two phenomena are, in fact, closely related. The application of technology has made both possible and necessary certain "economies of scale." The large capitalist enterprises and some nation-states have accordingly found it possible to penetrate and control the production process to an ever-increasing extent. While one could say that this tendency is nothing new, the fact is that the quantitative increases made possible by technology have resulted in a qualitatively new situation in which a relatively small number of huge transnational corporations (TNCs) are increasingly able to control economic life on a world scale. The exponential expansion of knowledge in our time has expanded the impact of economic decisions to virtually universal dimensions. The "unicentric" domination of the system (by Europe, the U.S., and more recently Japan) and the integration of economic affairs in the hands of single TNCs that control everything from the production of raw materials to the retailing of final products—and even the priority given to various sectors in the economy—have resulted in ever-widening inequalities of power and income.[6] No wonder that someone like Admiral Hyman B. Rickover, certainly no enemy of the capitalist system, can say:

> Political and economic power is increasingly being concentrated among a few large corporations and their officers—power they can apply against society, government, and individuals. Through their control of vast resources these large corporations have become, in effect, another branch of government. They often exercise the power of government, but without the checks and balances inherent in our democratic system. With their ability to dispense money, officials of large corporations may often exercise greater power to influence society than elected or appointed government officials—but without assuming any of the responsibilities and without being subject to public scrutiny. . . . The corporate officials who generate these pressures [to meet assigned corporate profit objectives] . . . are hidden behind the remote corporate screen and are rarely, if ever, held accountable for the results.[7]

Here again in the case of the TNCs we encounter a claim to "objectivity" that regards any interference with the total system as a utopian, arbitrary, and destructive disruption of "the nature of things," a breach of inviolable law. This law, regarded as synonymous with freedom, is ultimately identical with "the laws of the market," the commercial relations of liberal capitalism. A priest of the economic theory that undergirds this claim of the TNCs waxes mystical when he speaks of it: "The fundamental attitude of true individualism is one of *humility* toward the processes by which mankind has achieved things which have *not been designed or understood by any individual* and are indeed greater than individual minds."[8] "The invisible hand" of Adam Smith has finally grown powerful enough to universalize its operation, prevailing throughout the world and in every area of human life. As Hinkelammert says, it can now "judge over life and death but cannot itself be judged in terms of the effect it has on the life and death of every individual. . . . The market is elevated into the reason or logic of life and the intellect."⁹

It is a hoax, we said. But the trick easily succeeds. The most fundamental political decisions—about economy, education, use of resources, population policy, arms production—are presented as inviolable laws, as "the nature of things" or of "reality." The consequences of such laws are pronounced "inevitable."

We seem to have reached a point in the history of humankind, however, when the "inevitable consequences" of the so-called objective exigencies threaten to lead us to self-destruction. It may be necessary, therefore, to look again for that "master art" which, in Aristotle's view, was concerned with "the good of the community" and which, for him, belongs not merely to the sphere of instrumental reason but to that of virtue—that is, to the sphere of what is "fine and just." Or, in Habermas's words: "An energetic attempt must be made consciously to take in hand the mediation between technical progress and the conduct of life."¹⁰

A CHALLENGE FOR CHRISTIANS

The seriousness of our situation can hardly be exaggerated. Perhaps no one in recent times has given a more sober and at the same time more painful summary of the crisis than Robert Heilbroner in his justly famous *Inquiry Into the Human Prospect.* "There is a question in the air," he says: "Is there hope for man?" Heilbroner examines the internal and external threats that swirl around "the human future." He takes inventory of the economic, political, social, and moral resources on which we can draw to overcome our predicament, and then reaches this disheartening conclusion:

> The outlook for man, I believe, is painful, difficult, perhaps desperate, and the hope that can be held out for his human prospect seems to be very slim indeed. Thus, to anticipate the conclusions of our inquiry, the answer as to whether we can conceive of the future other than as a continuation of the darkness, cruelty, and disorder of the past seems to me to be no; and to the question of whether worse impends, yes.¹¹

Toward the end of the book, he repeats his bleak prognosis:

> If then, by the question "Is there hope for man?" we ask whether it is possible to meet the challenge of the future without the payment of a fearful price, the answer must be: "No, there is no such hope."¹²

Then he adds: "There is now nowhere to turn except to those private beliefs and disbeliefs that guide each of us through life."[13]

For us Christians this last sentence holds both challenge and temptation. "Beliefs and disbeliefs," convictions and ethical direction—is not that our particular field of competence? Are we not, as Pope Paul VI claimed at the United Nations Assembly, "experts in humanity"?

Four lines that we have begun to uncover pose for us a definite challenge: (1) Life has become socialized to such an extent that individual lives are nuclei determined by the crisscrossing of complex lines of economic, scientific-technological, communications, and cultural structures. There is therefore no individual prospect except as incorporated in a social prospect—which today must be worldwide in its dimensions. (2) This collective prospect is in our day a critical one. Violence seems to be erupting everywhere. In so many respects humankind exhibits an apparent inability, unwillingness, or impotence: to organize life on our earth on human terms; to use the resources of our world intelligently for the common good; to harness science in the service of a richer and fuller life; to subordinate bigness (more things, more power, greater wealth) to quality; to make of our diverse philosophical, political, and religious viewpoints an occasion for mutual encounter and enrichment; to structure an economy of solidarity rather than of destruction; to devise political structures able to cope with the problems and give viability to the hopes of our time. (3) An intense and resolute effort seems necessary if we are to bring this complex reality under human control and subordinate it to human ends. It cannot be left at the mercy of so-called objective "scientific-technological reason" or "economic laws" because such objectivity does not exist. Our task is to subordinate power to human decisions and human goals, and this is precisely the function of political ethics. (4) For us Christians this means that as we join in this human effort to articulate a political ethics for today's world we shoulder the task of bringing to bear upon it the basic "beliefs and disbeliefs that guide each of us [as Christians] through life." In other words, we are invited to elaborate a Christian ethics of politics.

But the challenge is also a temptation: It would be easy to embrace the idealistic fallacy that, since the gospel is the revelation of God's purpose for humankind, we can directly derive from the gospel a political ethics or, even worse, a political ideology and program. We may think we can dig up from our Christendom past some "social doctrine," dust it off and refurbish it, and offer it as a solution to our present problems. Like a spiritual "Superman," religion dashes to the rescue of our stranded societies. In the U.S., in areas of Europe, in Latin America, there is an increasing and vociferous chorus demanding that political decisions be determined on the basis of "Christian ethics." In fact, traditional defenders of a total separation between religion and politics have sometimes become ardent political activists in the name of the Christian faith.

What then should we do? We dare not let the urgency of the problem drive us into yielding to the temptation. But neither should fear of the temptation prevent us from accepting the challenge. We urgently need a Christian ethics of politics precisely in order that we may avoid a wrong politicization of Christianity. But, while we dare not forget the rich heritage of Christian ethics from times past—as elaborated in both Catholic and Protestant traditions—we can no longer work within the parameters (the presuppositions, the understandings of society, the views of nature and of human nature) that guided the articulation of those traditions. This has become increasingly clear. None other than the dean of American Christian political ethics John Bennett has recently sounded the call for a new social ethics that will be based on "a radical imperative" and yet related to the realities of our present situation.[14]

This is the task to which I would contribute—on the basis of our Christian history and experience in Latin America—some preliminary and tentative comments. It is necessarily an ecumenical task, both in the sense of demanding a worldwide perspective and the participation of Christians from a wide range of places and traditions and in the sense of drawing from the insights of diverse disciplines. Above all, it is a task that cannot be accomplished at a purely theoretical level but must be related to praxis—a praxis that is entered into and reflected on critically.

POLITICS, POWER, AND FREEDOM

What is the nature of the political question? How can we understand and analyze the phenomenon of political existence in order to relate it to our Christian understanding of the meaning and purpose of human life and history? What is "politics"?

Perhaps it was easier for Aristotle than for us to formulate a political ethics. For him, the basic elements—social classes, the nature of the state, the relation between the different forms of human sociability, economic organization—were all grounded in nature. Virtue was, to be sure, a state of character, a disposition to choose the right, the mean. But the actual content of political decision was determined by natural law.

The same conviction, theologically interpreted, proved serviceable to scholastic theologians throughout the Middle Ages. Ethics and politics might conflict in the actual conduct of the prince (even when he was a prince of the Church) but in theory they were one—written by the Creator himself into the very nature of human life, confirmed and clarified by revelation, and safeguarded and interpreted by the Church. There was only one thing to do—honor natural law! Occasional—or not so occasional—transgressions could be condemned, condoned, forgotten, or forgiven, but they could not be ethically justified.

As people of the Renaissance found the "natural law" arrangements of medieval times increasingly inadequate for meeting the political, social, and economic needs of the new age that was dawning, the discrepancies came to assume more and more the character of rule rather than exception. Toward the end of the fifteenth century Niccolò Machiavelli in *The Prince* dared to give explicit expression to the changed view:

> He who neglects what is done in order to follow what ought to be done will sooner learn how to ruin than how to preserve himself. . . . Wherefore it is necessary for a prince to harden himself and learn to be good, or otherwise, according to the exigence of his affairs. For if we consider things impartially we shall find some things which in appearance are virtuous, and yet, if pursued, would bring certain destruction; and others, on the contrary, that are seemingly bad, which if followed by a prince, procure his peace and security.[15]

The harshness of many of Machiavelli's maxims—that to be feared is better than to be loved, that the prince need not keep his word if it is disadvantageous to him—has created the image and reputation of an amoral and unprincipled politics. Machiavelli has been interpreted as a realist, a monster, a nationalist, the creator of the science of politics, and a satirist of his times. In any case, he laid down a couple basic premises for all subsequent reflection on political ethics, namely, the autonomy of politics and the fact of power. "It is known," writes Benedetto Croce, "that Machiavelli discovers the necessity and autonomy of politics, of politics which is beyond or, rather, below moral good and evil, which has its own laws against which it is useless to rebel."[16] Machiavelli, says Max Lerner, wrote "a grammar of power, not only for the sixteenth century, but for the ages that have followed."[17]

More than a century after Machiavelli's death Hobbes's *Leviathan* would articulate in classical form an understanding of "the matter, form, and authority of government"—that is, politics in a more specific way—that would try to spell out this "grammar of power." Hobbes can also speak of "nature," but for him nature is not "an instinct of sociability inborn in all human beings" (Cicero) or an innate sense of justice, but the individual existence turned to the quest of its own egoistic interests, which—in a state of nature—means "the war of all against all." Hobbes is thus, consciously and explicitly, the very anti-thesis of Aristotle. The *polis* for him is not the result of a natural sociability or a quest for the common good, but a sort of "contract" through which human beings resign their authority to a "sovereign" in order to be protected from "the others."

Thus power (*potestas*) is the constitutive element of political exist-ence. The law, therefore, is an embodiment not of natural justice but of the will of the sovereign; the sovereign—whether an individual or a group—is himself above all law, "free from any norm or rule." The "multitude" of the people no longer constitutes a political fact; it "becomes" political when it is unified and coordinated. Only power can do that, and thus generate "this great Leviathan which is called 'repub-lic' or 'state.'"[18] Thus, to quote Lebrun, "There is no community without unification, there is no unification without sovereignty; but there is also no sovereignty without absolute and perpetual power," that is, power which is not subject to any other authority and which is exercised without interruption.[19]

Does this mean that there are no universal values and no ethical laws? In the new world that emerged from the time of Machiavelli on-wards—the world of the new states, of the bourgeoisie, of capital-ism—will power be the only reality and self-interest, the only basis of political existence? Is the demise of natural law also the end of ethics? Hobbes was immediately accused and attacked on these grounds. From his peers in the rival university of Cambridge to Rousseau, Locke, and Kant, he was blamed for subordinating law to power, thus endangering human freedom and opening the way to absolutism and tyranny. It would not be difficult to show that such criticisms are only partially justified. Without compromising his political philosophy, Hobbes was quite careful to introduce into his thinking certain limits and purposes in the exercise of power. But we are more interested here in underscor-ing his basic thrust: however conceived or explained, *power* is at the base of any political entity. Liberal ideologues are unable to escape this fact of power. Even Kant had to admit that no ethical community—no community of ethical subjects derived from that universal moral im-perative which is innate in us all—could exist empirically without "unity in a common submission to an external, legal coercion."

For the liberals, though, power must be subordinate to freedom. For Locke, the absolute right of private property is both the heart and the guarantee of freedom. It establishes both the function of the state—to protect this right—and its limits—state action must stop before this inviolable "sign and sacrament" of individuality. Power is thus exercised for the sake of freedom and must be reduced to a minimum in order to enlarge the realm of individual liberty.

Kant, on the other hand, would look for a deeper and universal foundation for ethics. He asks two basic questions: "What ought I to do?" and "What may I hope for?" The answer to the first question is "the categorical imperative," man's a priori moral sense which demands that we act as if "the maxim of your action were to become through your will a universal law of nature" or, more concretely, "that you never treat humanity . . . merely as a means but always at the same time as an end." The answer to the second question is "the kingdom of ends" or "kingdom of God," where humanity is always treated as an end, where virtue and happiness are one. Thus, a new world of meaning and value emerges, an ethics which is not an objective order "out there," within the reach of "pure reason," but a subjective order in the individual conscience, where it is perceived by "practical reason."

Kant's was an admirable achievement. But we have already hinted at the great difficulty he experienced in trying to relate this "ethical community of ends" to the concrete historical problems of political existence; so difficult was the connection that he had to admit the need for an absolute power in order to establish the external conditions that would enable the ethical community to exist.

Herein lies the frightful price that the modern world has had to pay for the recovery of ethics. All of modern philosophy has been built on the insurmountable separation between man and world, between subject and object, between human consciousness and external reality. Kant's reconstruction took place within the framework of this presupposition: ethics would belong henceforth to the private and inner realm. Any public, objective ethics could be only the spillover of the individual conscience. Out there in the external world of objective structures the order of power had an autonomy and direction of its own. Liberals would see it as an unavoidable nuisance, a threat to individual freedom, and would therefore advocate a progressive weakening of the state, the dissolution of power—a dissolution that would be automatically proportionate to the growth of individual initiative, rights, and freedom. Hegel, on the contrary, could see in the state the historical embodiment of the spirit's pilgrimage toward freedom, and therefore as in some way the "incarnation" of the ethical community Kant was seeking.

We shall have occasion—in chapter 7 from a theological perspective—to return to the discussion of this dialectics of power and freedom. Our limited purpose here has been not to trace the history of political thought, but only to remind ourselves of the way in which the problem of political ethics was posed at the beginning of the modern era. It is against this background that Christianity has had to face the challenge: Is a Christian political ethics at all possible, one that will be operative in the public sphere? In this world of power, of economic relations and structures, a world that maintains its autonomy and will not yield to voluntaristic moral ideals imposed from the outside, a world in which power and freedom seem to pull in opposite directions—what can Christians say and do? How can Christianity respond to the new practice and the new conceptions of political life in the modern world?

2

Christian Responses to the Ethical Dilemma

Three years after the publication of Machiavelli's *The Prince,* an English humanist gave expression to a totally opposite conception of society. In *Utopia,* Thomas More's hero Raphael tells of a wonderful place where force is never used and Christian principles rule supreme. Twenty years later More's execution for resisting the concentration of power in the hands of Henry VIII bore witness to the fact that utopian projects would not fare well in the new age that was dawning. What happens when Christian faith comes up against the question of power? Are compromise or martyrdom the only alternatives? Ernst Troeltsch, commenting on this dilemma, ends on a confession of faith:

> Only through faith, hope, and love can the *bellum omnium contra omnes,* to which nature and egoism incline us, be overcome. That is the inmost meaning of the Christian gospel, although this same gospel has always known well enough that the task thus set to us poor little men is far more difficult than any merely rationalistic optimism is ever willing to admit.[1]

Such a confession, though, has to be articulated theologically so that Christians—however frail our efforts—may contribute to the triumph of faith, hope, and love over egoism and conflict.

We would like now to explore some of the ways in which Christians, from the perspective of faith, have tried to respond to the challenge of power. Our purpose at this point is neither to trace the history of Christian political ethics nor to discuss it in detail but simply to characterize briefly some typical approaches to the theological concerns that will later engage our attention.

THE "TWO KINGDOMS"

On the question of "how secular authority is to be harmonized with the gospel" Martin Luther disagreed with Johann von Schwarzenberg, the eminent jurist of his time. We do not know what von Schwarzenberg had written on the subject, but we do know Luther's response—

Temporal Authority: To What Extent It Should Be Obeyed (1523).[2] This treatise provides the fullest expression of what has come to be known as Luther's doctrine of the "two kingdoms" (or two governments)—the first Protestant understanding of a "political ethics." The idea of two realms of power had taken many forms throughout the Middle Ages, from Augustine's two cities—which Luther explicitly acknowledges as his inspiration—to the "two swords" or "two luminaries" developed by thirteenth-century canonists. Luther's problem and intention was, nevertheless, a different one. In his view, a fatal confusion had taken place: ecclesiastical authorities, in the name of the church, had become earthly rulers, while secular powers were claiming authority in spiritual matters.[3]

The reformer does more than simply try to settle a jurisdictional problem; he develops a theological understanding that has had deep impact on Protestant political ethics ever since. Luther's concept of the two kingdoms is, as Bornkamm puts it, "tri-dimensional." It refers to the distinction between church and state, the dialectical relation of law and gospel, and the twofold character of each individual in the world—as both "private" person and "public" person.

Leaving aside the scholarly discussions and the heated controversies that have taken place around this two-kingdoms doctrine, I would like to underline three aspects that have an important bearing on our present theme: (1) Luther discerns the signs of the times when he recognizes the relative autonomy of political power and existence. While he may vacillate in the matter of appealing to "reason," to "natural law," and in some cases even to expediency, he realizes that the "secular kingdom" cannot be arbitrarily subject to a heteronomous authority, be it that of church or biblical law or some idealistic principle. (2) Moreover, Luther has a positive conception of political power. He rejects any retreat into a spiritual isolation that would abdicate responsibility for this more ambiguous and dark sphere of the world. Political power, for Luther, falls within the sphere of God's sovereignty and providence, and hence the Christian, whether prince or subject, has to serve God in the political sphere as well as in the Christian community. (3) Luther carries the distinction between the two "cities" over into the existence of each Christian person. He does this, however, by means of a distinction that will eventually play readily into one of the most cherished notions to be developed by the modern bourgeois world—the distinction between "private" and "public," with the former referring to the gospel and the latter to a law the contents of which is not clearly defined.

It is this latent—and sometimes not so latent—dualism which, carried over rigidly into the relations of church and state and the relation of personal life and public life, would eventually bring into being certain consequences that would call into question the whole doctrine of the two kingdoms. The use of this dualism to justify the absolute claims of political power and to champion an almost blind acceptance of "the powers that be" runs through much of later history—and not only in Germany, not only in Lutheranism. The darkest page of this history, no doubt, is the use of a theology of "the orders" by many a theologian during the period of Hitler's National Socialism. Even a theologian as alert and discerning as Paul Althaus fell into the trap of using this distinction between "public" and "private" to supply a Christian justification of Nazi ideology.[4] In this respect, however harsh it may have been, we can well understand Karl Barth's indictment of such an approach:

> The German people suffers from the heritage of a paganism that is mystical. . . . And it suffers too from the heritage of the greatest Christian of Germany, from Martin Luther's error on the relation between law and gospel, between the temporal and the spiritual order and power. This error has established, confirmed, and idealized the natural paganism of the German people instead of limiting and restraining it.[5]

Is it fair to lay such grave accusations at the doorstep of Martin Luther? Does the doctrine of the two kingdoms necessarily pave the way for this radical dualism that emancipates political power from the demands of the gospel, even from God's revealed will and purpose? I can think of no better response than that of Gustaf Wingren on this issue.[6] Like many other modern students of the question, Wingren establishes clearly that for Luther both kingdoms—the secular and the spiritual—are under God's sovereignty and both are expressions of God's love. The difference lies not in a supposed autonomy of the secular in relation to God but in the fact that God rules in the secular kingdom through "the law and the sword" and in the spiritual kingdom through "the gospel and the Spirit." In both spheres, moreover, God's love is locked in struggle with the destructive power of the enemy, and the Christian cannot remain neutral in this battle. The connection between the two kingdoms, between *justitia civilis* and *justitia christiana,* is established "vertically" by the unity of God's purpose and love operative in both, and "horizontally" through Christian love, the concrete expression of which is one's "vocation."

In the exercise of their secular vocations Christians, working through the structures of society, can give expression to their love for the neighbor. To the question of the autonomy of politics, therefore, the answer is Christian vocation—"vocation's work as divine love coming down to earth, the same love that was in Christ."[7] Thus, at the ethical level gospel and law, power and love, come together in the life of individual Christians, in whatever *Stand* (social or vocational location) they may find themselves in society.

We should not be surprised to find in Luther this particular answer to the political question. For Luther in fact (could this be an unconscious anticipation of the subjective individualism that would later capture Protestant piety?) "the world and the masses are and always will be un-Christian."[8] But even if we leave aside this question about the piety of the masses, we are still confronted with a serious problem: Do Christians have any guidance as to what is that "good of the neighbor" which we are supposed to pursue in society? We have already pointed to Luther's hesitation and to his vacillation in appealing now to man's moral conscience, now to natural law, and now to reason. Wingren concludes that a guide of this sort "cannot be named," because we would thereby fall under yet another "law." Consequently, as some Luther scholars have pointed out, vocation tends to become a fixed and rigid structure determined by the prevailing social and political institutions; thus the existing secular order determines the concrete course of Christian love. "Love of neighbor," so far as the political order is concerned, has thereby become captive to the dominant political structure. Its explosive evangelical power—think of the parable of the good Samaritan—has thus been tamed. Political ethics then becomes a rather formal "mandate," the concrete content of which is autonomously determined by "the world." Love merely does honestly and well what the system demands. Passive disobedience seems to be the only critical possibility open—and then, only when a clearly (explicitly and not only implicitly) "religious question" is at stake.[9] History, unfortunately, offers all too many painful illustrations of what this can mean—and not always among Lutherans.

CHRISTIAN PRINCIPLES?

We come back to the question raised by the new conception of power and politics: In the new world that emerged from the time of Machiavelli onwards, will power be the only reality? Are there no universal values, no ethical law? Is the demise of natural law also the end of ethics? In the eighteenth and nineteenth centuries a new answer begins to emerge along lines that we could call idealistic—with no pejorative meaning intended.

We have already pointed to the significance of Immanuel Kant's struggle to reestablish an ethical authority rooted in man's subjective moral consciousness. Protestant political ethics was built for the most part on the presupposition of this distinction (in fact separation) between a public sphere and a private sphere—a distinction that was actually operative in Protestant lands long before it had found philosophical and theological articulation. We have just spoken of how interpretations of the two-kingdoms doctrine tended to consign gospel-love to the private realm and give over the public sphere to a "law" the contents of which remained undefined—and hence were determined ultimately by the will of the "authority" (the powers that be).

Liberal social ethics, a kind of precursor of the American "Social Gospel," developed in the second half of the nineteenth century along neo-Kantian lines. Here too, the categorical imperative (and its social correlate, the kingdom of God) was translated in terms of love—the fatherhood of God, the brotherhood of men, and the infinite value of the human soul, according to Adolf von Harnack's classic interpretation. It is instructive to hear Harnack on the role of the church in society. We quote from a beautiful paper in which, without hiding his commitment to a social-democratic program, he advocates an active role for Christians in society:

> Therefore Protestants believe that if the government exercises its power rightly, it will be at one with *the ethical ideals of Christianity,* and accordingly, the ordering of temporal affairs must safely be left in its hands. But this in no way debars the church from raising its voice in protest *against moral and social evils,* and from influencing both public opinion and the conduct of *matters of national interest.*[10]

But then, when we ask what this means in specific terms, we get the following answer:

> The more stress is laid upon this, the more need there is to define the limits within which the church must confine its activity—bounds which do not include economic questions. It has nothing to do with such *practical questions* of social-economics as the nationalization of private property and enterprises, land-tenure reforms, restrictions of legal hours of work, price regulations, taxation, and insurance.[11]

What, then, does belong within the competence of the church?

> It is the duty of the church to interfere in public conditions wherever it finds that *serious moral evils* are being tolerated . . . dueling . . . a state of things destructive of the sanctity of marriage and of family life . . . where weak are trodden underfoot . . . language that, in the name of Christianity, destroys

the peace of the land and sows scorn and hatred broadcast . . . to draw together the rich and the poor . . . to help break down mischievous class prejudices.[12]

I have included these lengthy quotations from Harnack because we meet here the clearest expression of serious, committed, bourgeois Christian views in the Kantian tradition. Harnack's is not the voice of conservatism. The power of the whole liberal tradition is here expressed—a firm adherence to Christian ethical principles, a concern for justice and the weak, a call to a stern morality. But the limitation is also clear—the ethical principles belong to a different world from that in which the actual structural decisions are made. Christian principles and moral conviction are what the church can contribute, whereas socio-economic and political questions move in a different sphere, an autonomous technical realm in which a quite different epistemological principle—"technical knowledge"—holds sway.

Even before Harnack had articulated this interpretation of the role of the church in society, Karl Marx was writing his sharp criticism of this idealistic-Christian-bourgeois social ethics. We know of his violent and caustic rejection of Christian love, Christian social principles, and Christian socialism. The reason for this rejection is simple: Christianity has done no good and can do no good because it moves at a level of "fantasy" and "projection" which results only in justifying things as they are rather than changing them.

Thus for instance love, according to Marx, is "the source of Christian statecraft." But in capitalistic society it is money alone—not love—that gives significance to human relationships: "Human individuality, human morality, has become both an article of commerce and the form in which money exists."[13] As long as human relations are mediated by money, as long as human life is alienated from the concrete individual and "objectivized" in a "fetish," real love is only a dream, a fiction, "a fantasized expression of the existing world." Or take the matter of Christian principles: they speak about justice, about the condition of the poor. However, "they preach cowardice, self-abasement, resignation, submission, and humility" while what the proletariat needs is "courage, confidence, pride, and independence even more than it needs its daily bread." "The social principles of Christianity are sneaking and hypocritical whilst the proletariat is revolutionary."[14] It is true that Christian socialists also speak about the fetishism of money and about a proletariat revolution. But they confuse everything by "theologizing economic and political issues." To be sure, they speak of "overthrowing

Mammon"—money—but *how* "we are not informed." Thus, their
revolution becomes merely an insurrection, deprived of scientific basis;
in other words, the moral conscience is unrelated to a rational understanding of concrete reality. The only possible result of such a failure is
an "ideology," an inverted picture of reality under which existent
reality is both hidden and justified. The "ethical individual" of the
Kantian tradition is an abstraction that hides the real human beings
who are actually engaged in the material process of producing and
reproducing human life. Just as in abstract politics, we are offered a
fantastic choreography that does not change the realities of human
life.[15]

FROM PRINCIPLE TO PROGRAM— THE SEARCH FOR AN ECUMENICAL SOCIAL ETHICS

We may or may not agree with the Marxian critique of idealistic
Christian ethics. But we cannot ignore the question implied in Marx's
criticism: You Christians speak of justice and love, of transforming the
world and vindicating the right of the poor—but *how* "we are not
informed." When it comes to matters of morality can Christians contribute something more than simply general principles, or norms for
individuals?

The question became a pressing one for Christian churches in Europe
and North America during the crisis precipitated for the modern world
by World War I. The "Life and Work" movement was their more
conspicuous attempt to face the question. Space does not allow us here
to survey the whole history of ecumenical social thought vis-à-vis the
questions raised by the reconstruction of Europe following World War
I, the challenge of Nazism, and the new shape of the world that emerged
after World War II.[16] But it may prove significant for our reflection to
point out some of the lines along which ecumenical thought has moved,
particularly since the World Council of Churches came into being in
1948.

The political frame of reference at the time was the cold war. An
ecumenical movement that intended to include both Eastern and Western churches could hardly identify itself with only one side in the
conflict. Internally, the theological concern had to be to overcome
whatever dualism might prevent the churches from saying a significant
word in the world of political reality.

The theological points of departure were not the same for all. While
theologians in the U.S. tended to build on the basis of an anthropology
that combined the ethos of the Social Gospel with Niebuhrian "Chris-

tian realism," Europeans had rediscovered the significance of eschatology both as a call to ethical action in society and as a caveat against utopianism. But within these divergent frames of references, some common basic features are easily discernible.

Both in Europe and in America there is a twofold front. On the one hand, against conservatism and inertia, ecumenical thought emphasizes the changeability of human structures; as a result it issues a call to responsibility for active participation in social change. On the other hand, there is a warning against any attempt to erect a "tower of Babel"—a warning that can be sounded both externally against Marxist utopianism and internally against illusions about building the kingdom of God on earth.

Such "realism" is immediately confronted by the question concerning criteria for action in the world. If one intends to avoid falling back on abstract "Christian principles," it is necessary to find "historical mediations" between Christian "ideals" and the concrete social problems. One of the most important notions articulated in this direction was that of "middle axioms" sketched at Oxford already in 1938. By combining several formulations one can understand "middle axioms" as moving in three concentric circles of increasing concretization:

(1) There are some basic ethical principles, a kind of natural law—or, perhaps better, a moral common sense in a Kantian sense—on which there is a virtually universal consensus: that goods and benefits must be justly distributed, that there must be equal opportunity for all, that a measure of freedom is necessary for human development, that honesty and truthfulness are needed in our common life. Christians not only share such principles with other human beings; they also offer a specific motivation for putting them into practice—Christian love—and a firm foundation for establishing their validity—God's will.

(2) These general principles can be specified in terms of certain criteria for political action: (a) the welfare of all, including material, cultural, and political conditions for human development and a measure of security; (b) freedom, which is tested in the liberty of minorities to dissent, space for the existence of voluntary association, and freedom of expression; (c) order, the peace and cooperation between different groups and sectors of society that prevents destructive conflicts between classes and interests; and (d) justice, in the sense of the *suum cuique* understood as equality of opportunity.

(3) In particular historical circumstances the application of these four criteria requires a recognition of their interrelatedness, analysis of the concrete circumstances, and the correct use of available means. In this way some immediate goals can be defined—middle axioms in a new

sense: in the present situation for instance (c. 1955–60), the prevention
of nuclear war; racial integration; the prevention of extensive unemployment; cooperation between the state, economic interests, and
labor; and self-determination for peoples who have been under colonial
domination. Christians, to be sure, are not asked to establish a political
platform of their own or to organize a Christian political party, but by
way of these middle axioms they are provided with some operative
criteria for their participation in political life.

Starting from an eschatological perspective that underscores the universal lordship of Christ (in this respect echoing a criticism which
Reformed theologians had directed against the two-kingdoms doctrine)
and the unity of individual and social, of personal and structural reality
implied in the eschatological goal, the German theologian Heinz-
Dietrich Wendland sought a concept which would offer a better synthetic vision than the operative idea of middle axioms. Over against the
"absolute" utopia of Marxist or Christian "enthusiasm," he speaks of a
"real" utopia (sometimes in the sense of "realistic," sometimes in the
sense of "relative"). The central notion of love, which for Wendland
expresses the inner content of both the kingdom of God and natural
law, is the "global goal" of all human construction. This goal can be
described in other terms as "a society worthy of human beings," a
"humanized" society in which human dignity and the economic and
social well-being of the individual and of the whole society are
adequately promoted. The more concrete definitions of this general goal
run along lines that are closely parallel to those of the middle axioms
already discussed.

The "responsible society" model offered to the ecumenical movement a valuable instrument for facing the problems posed by the social
and political dilemmas of the developed world, but the new questions
and contradictions introduced into the ecumenical debate by the growing presence of churches from the so-called Third World soon began to
challenge this mediating position. A new appreciation on the part of the
Asian countries (particularly India) of the role of the state engaged in
"nation building" called into question the almost exclusively negative
attitude toward nationalism that had hitherto been predominant in
ecumenical thinking. The new African states that were seeking a national identity under the leadership of their charismatic leaders, and
later the Latin American analyses in terms of domination and dependence further sharpened the criticism. The Geneva Conference on
Church and Society in 1966 crystalized the challenge. The criticisms
arising in this connection can best be summarized under four points.

First, the question of power and the role of the state, somewhat in the background since Oxford, was again brought to the fore—this time by those who felt that the issue was not a "balancing" of power but a revolutionary transferring of power to the deprived and dominated classes and nations. The obsession with formal democracy, they felt, could not always accommodate the urgency of the need for rapid social change. "Social revolution," wrote Richard Shaull, one of the stronger spokespersons for this position, "seems, therefore, to be the main problem to which our generation must find a solution."[17] The theology of the kingdom began to take on new significance and, without returning to the naive optimism of some kinds of Social Gospel, Shaull himself could say that "Christians may perceive, in certain situations, a relative coincidence of direction between the revolutionary struggle and God's humanizing action in the world."[18]

Second, there was an emphasis on a contextual approach. This was coupled with considerable diffidence of universal principles, affirmations in which it was often easy to discover the concerns and interests of the "dominant center" (Europe and the U.S.).

Third, while ecumenical social thinking had taken a negative view of ideology, the new countries and classes engaged in a revolutionary struggle insisted that ideology can also be understood in a positive sense. The official report of the theological commission clearly summarizes this point of view: "By ideology we mean a process quite different from a total system of ideas which is closed to correction and new insight. Ideology, as we use it here, is the theoretical and analytical structure of thought which undergirds successful action either to realize the revolutionary change in society or to undergird and justify the status quo."[19]

Finally, there was an emphasis on praxis as the necessary presupposition of any significant Christian social ethics. Konrad Reiser expresses it well: "For ecumenical social thought this has meant that research and reflection have become intimately related to areas of active involvement."[20]

This fourfold correction amounted to a radical shift. While the "responsible society" was predicated on the basis of a stable society which, through democratic procedures, endeavored to realize a fair degree of social justice, the new forces were struggling for a new and just society. They called for a radical shift in power, a mobilizing vision (ideology), a total commitment (praxis), and a concrete historical focus (contextuality).

The Uppsala Assembly (1968) took up the Geneva challenge and launched a process that has been singularly fruitful—and controversial. As a result of this process over the last fifteen years the World Council of

Churches has felt the challenge to design a vision of the new society toward which we intend to move. This attempt to envision the "just, participatory, and sustainable society" called for by the Nairobi Assembly (1975), which would combine the three basic demands felt to be priority items, has led to the growing conviction that justice must become the primary focus of such a vision, and that a political ethics is an indispensable instrument for the struggle.[21]

CHRISTIAN SOCIAL DOCTRINE—AN ETHICS WORTHY OF HUMAN BEINGS

Even in such a limited and sketchy survey we cannot forgo giving an account of Roman Catholic "social doctrine." This complex and elaborate body of doctrine has its roots in the medieval notions of natural law; we, however, are particularly interested in the "social doctrine of the Church" developed during the last hundred years in response to the challenge of the social conditions of the modern world, the so-called social question. For our present purposes I shall limit myself to a few remarks about the continuities and discontinuities in this development.

While Protestantism has usually tried to build its ethics on a specifically Christian basis—and consequently has often had difficulty relating it to the "autonomous" spheres of public life—Catholicism tries to ground its ethical pronouncements in a comprehensive philosophy that spans the gap between revelation and reason, between church and world. More precisely, it builds on an anthropology that finds in the "natural sociability" of the human being the foundation for all social ethics. The traditional notions of natural law, however, have been sharply criticized for their tendency to "sacralize" structures and arrangements which reflect concrete historical conditions and particular social systems. Consequently, we find in Roman Catholic pronouncements a tendency to move away from defining specific norms—for family, property, authority—as "natural laws." Instead, there is a tendency to derive such norms from a personalistic anthropology through "mediating concepts" (such as the concept of personality and the principles of solidarity, the common good and subsidiarity), concepts that are considered necessary for personal human fulfillment and in turn normative for the ordering of the institutions and relations of society. In the Vatican II "Pastoral Constitution on the Church in the Modern World" and the encyclicals of Paul VI and John Paul II the term "natural law" has all but disappeared and been replaced by this personalistic anthropology.

On the other hand, a comparison between nineteenth-century encyclicals and the more recent ones shows also the increasing influence of the biblical and theological emphases of the last fifty years. While the philosophical foundation is still present, biblical references have ceased to be mere "proof texts" and have become instead a coherent argument about God's purpose and will as revealed in the history of salvation. A christological and biblical humanism (as in John Paul II's *Redemptor Hominis*) supports and strengthens philosophical personalism. Thus, recent Roman Catholic pronouncements frequently parallel ecumenical statements of the WCC on such subjects as human dignity, peace, and the struggle against poverty.

Moreover, the reluctance to develop a casuistry for political and economic questions on the basis of natural law has stimulated the quest for a different "mediation" to the concrete and particular. Hence the growing place given to scientific social analysis—for instance, of the causes of underdevelopment in *Populorum Progressio,* or of the problems of modern economy in *Laborens Exercens.*

The "dialogical" method inaugurated in the Vatican Constitution *Gaudium et Spes,* where successive sections try to analyze a given theme empirically and then reflect on it theologically, has become dominant in Catholic social ethics, "Christian social doctrine," writes Josef Höffner, "encompasses objective scientific disciplines and normative ones derived from philosophical and theological methods applied to the public sphere."[22] Social analysis, however, is not only an instrument for casuistic definition but also a means to grasp a total situation, and thus a necessary step toward "discerning the signs of the times," that is, toward understanding a particular historical time in the context of God's purpose and action.

When we arrive at this point we are not far from the concerns that moved the WCC meetings of Geneva and Uppsala. In the critical times in which we live—our lives challenged and urged by the conflicts and contradictions of a progressively unified and divided world—Christian social doctrine cannot rest content with having enunciated general principles or offered piecemeal objective solutions. It has to find a "prophetic" word—a word that rings with the authenticity of God's proclamation in Jesus Christ while also addressing the reality of human historical existence. While Catholic political ethics continues to maintain its traditional roots, it is clearly developing more and more in this direction.

DEFENSELESS RESISTANCE

Vicit Agnus Noster, eum sequamur—"Our Lamb has conquered; Him let us follow." With these words the Mennonite theologian John Howard Yoder begins and ends a book.[23] In it he argues cogently and persuasively for a Christian political ethics rooted in what has been variously called the radical, left-wing, enthusiastic, or sectarian tradition of Reformation times. In the decisive decade of 1520–30, while Luther was struggling to achieve a theological understanding and a political-ecclesiastical organization of the movement he had almost unawares set in motion, another vision and praxis was simultaneously emerging. Its proponents wished to push what they regarded as the timid and hesitant biblical and ecclesial understanding and praxis of the Reformers to their "radical consequences." Yoder points to five constitutive elements of this tradition: a critique of power, a sense of the meaning of suffering, a search for authenticity, a visible and voluntary community, and a universal vision.[24] He claims that this alternative "political ethics" is at one and the same time biblical, contemporary to Jesus, and still relevant for us.

Contrary to the dominant tendency in the conservative evangelical circles (to which most of the churches stemming from this Anabaptist tradition are related in the U.S.) Yoder claims that the ministry and message of Jesus are through and through political—related to society, to the present time, and to the question of power. Several decisive steps in his argument are worth noting.

In the first place, the political dimension of Jesus' mission is not derivative (as if it were a political consequence of general ethical principles) or accidental (as if Jesus had been caught in the particularities of a situation and wrongly understood as proclaiming a political message); it is the heart of his mission: "Jesus was, in his divinely mandated . . . prophethood, priesthood, and kingship, the bearer of a new possibility of human, social, and therefore political relationships."[25] The nature of those relationships is to be found in the concrete requirements of justice—redistribution of power and property and restoration of relationships of the "jubilee year"—that Jesus proclaims. Such demands are neither utopian dreams nor general principles but concrete "jubilee ordinances" to be "put into practice here and now" (at the time of Jesus' proclamation), and they are still fully relevant to our own time.

The inauguration of this new order was conceived not as an event outside of time, or at the end of time, but as the result of that particular intervention of God which sets human history—history here on earth with all its social relations—on a new track. In the effort to bring about such a society Jesus rejects the use of violence or political wisdom and chooses instead the way of "defenseless resistance."

> The one temptation the man Jesus faced—and faced again and again—as a
> constitutive element of his public ministry was the temptation to exercise

social responsibility, in the interest of justified revolution, through the use of available violent methods. Social withdrawal was no temptation to him. . . . Any alliance with the Sadducean establishment in the exercise of *conservative* social responsibility . . . was likewise excluded from the outset. We understand Jesus only if we can empathize with the threefold rejection: the self-evident, axiomatic, sweeping rejection of both quietism and establishment responsibility, and the difficult, constantly reopened, genuinely attractive option of the crusade.[26]

This path—the path of the cross—is the only legitimate way open to the disciple. In a survey of several levels and blocks of the New Testament tradition, Yoder shows that the apostolic conception of Christ's lordship (his victory over all "powers") and the apostolic ethics of conformity to Jesus Christ both point in the same direction: not toward indifference or conservatism but toward the costly "revolutionary subordination," refusing to accept the "order" of this world (which would be implied by entering the game of "power politics"), confronting dominion with servanthood and hostility with forgiveness, and thus exercising the same kind of "power" as that which triumphed in the Cross.

The "subject" of this kind of witness is not the isolated individual Christian but the witnessing community which in itself enacts and collectively portrays to the world the nature of this new order:

What needs to be seen is . . . that the primary social structure through which the gospel works to change other structures is that of the Christian community. Here, within this community, men are rendered humble and changed in the way they behave, not simply by a proclamation directed to their sense of guilt but also by genuine social relationships to other persons who ask them about their obedience."[27]

Yoder's position is not a mere reiteration of traditional pacifism but a polemic against traditional theological-ethical interpretations. According to Yoder, (1) these interpretations try to evade the direct implications of Jesus' political ethics of defenseless resistance either by confining it to an "interim status" in view of the "imminent" apocalyptic hopes, or by spiritualizing it, or by applying it only to the individual; or (2) they confine it to the realm of general principles which are then applied through social "mediations" in which the concrete demands of Jesus are lost; or (3) they supplement it by a "natural" or "historical" revelation that leads in the end to the same result—some form of dualism in which the ethics of Jesus is seen as irrelevant or inapplicable to political life.

We shall have occasion in due course to return to a consideration of

this question of the church's response to political power.[28] Suffice it here
to say that in view of the long history of the church it is difficult to see
how the church can avoid coming to grips with the concrete issues and
options of the outside world—and even if it could, it would still have to
face the questions of power and injustice within the community itself!
Moreover, as the community continues to be involved in the whole
nexus of social relations and conditions of public life in general, it
cannot avoid participating in the struggle of ideologies and powers now
taking place in the world. Yoder, naturally, is not unaware of these
facts. Yet, the very radicalness of his hermeneutical choice seems practically to foreclose such discussion from the outset.

Thus Christians over the ages have struggled in many different ways
to respond positively to an imperative—the concern and responsibility
for the shape and health of human society—that seems deeply rooted in
the very nature of the biblical message, so deeply rooted that no attempt
to ignore it or make it disappear by sleight of hand can be successful. Yet
the problems persist, stubbornly resistant to easy solutions. The hard
reality of power refuses to submit to general principles or moral norms.
Politics reveals an autonomy that has to be recognized and respected
unless one is willing to forgo efficacy altogether. No retreat into subjectivity, individualism, or otherworldliness can finally satisfy the Christian conscience. Yet theologically and spiritually, one is forced to hold
together under the one God this realm of power and the radical demand
of the Cross. Too sharp a distinction between the two kingdoms seems
to lead to a blind acceptance of "the powers that be" from which the
gospel is excluded, while an exclusive concentration on the way of
the cross seems to lead either to isolation or to utopianism. Can grace
and truth, justice and peace really meet? Is it possible to hold together
love and power, justice and order—not only in thought but also in
praxis and reality? In some such way is the problem of a Christian
political ethics posed for us by the history of the church's thought and
experience.

3

From Praxis to Theory and Back

Almost everybody knows—at least by name—the monumental work of Ernst Troeltsch on *The Social Teaching of the Christian Churches*. Few, however, will remember the incident that prompted him to write it. Troeltsch was invited to review a book authored by Nathusius on *Cooperation of the Church in the Solution of the Social Question*. He found it "an awful book." Churches, he agreed, were rightly concerned with the social question. But Nathusius's attempt and the similar attempts of so many others suffered from a "confusion of thought": (1) They thought they could move directly from the church as a community to society as a whole, and apply to the latter the criteria of the former. (2) They ignored the real nature of society—the relation of infrastructure to superstructure, the socioeconomic determinations, the nature of the state. (3) They were not aware of the ways in which society influenced Christian thought and ethics. Thus they naively supposed that "if they form an organization which expresses the love that flows from God and returns to him once more, they are also meeting the need of the social groups which make up humanity as a whole."[1]

What then should be done? Troeltsch responds:

> The question of the inward influence of Christianity upon the sense of personality, and upon ethical mutual relationships is certainly of immense importance . . . but . . . the only method for attempting to find an answer at all is by investigating the concrete effect of its influence in different social groups. In the course of such investigation, however, it will become evident that great tracts of social life, like that of the economic social order, throw a great deal of light upon the general fundamental tendency of Christian sociology, which permits us to draw certain inferences about the general character and the effect on civilization of Christian sociological principles.[2]

We may object to Troeltsch's excessive dependence on Max Weber's sociological categories and theory or be dissatisfied with his way of correlating sociological investigation and systematic theology. But Christian ethicists would have been wiser if they had taken more seriously his methodological advice—and example—of elaborating their ethical conclusions on the basis of careful sociohistorical analysis.

We may, however, raise the question: When we are dealing with what actually *happens* or *has happened,* with forms of Christian political praxis, is such analysis still ethics? Can we speak of ethics at all unless we are asking the normative question: How *should* Christians *have acted* and how *should* they *act* politically? Ethics is a normative discipline; it cannot be reduced to mere description. How are we to relate the normative and descriptive approaches?

The question depends on two other related questions: First, what is the place of ethics in the relation between facts and ideas, reality and consciousness—which is the question of idealism and realism—and second, how can we relate praxis (both secular and Christian) and theory (both socioanalytical and theological)? These are the methodological questions we must now face, questions which in turn force us to reach for models and categories that do not belong to the traditional baggage of theology.

In the present chapter I shall try to state my presuppositions and clarify my categories in dialogue with the human sciences, a dialogue that will claim attention throughout the inquiry. The exposition will be organized around four main topics: (1) the relation between facts and ideas, the problem of objectivity; (2) the relation of socioanalytical tools and research to theological-ethical reflection; (3) the relation between Christian and secular social praxis and theological theory; (4) theoretical models for the analysis of society. Needless to say, the intention is not to offer here an extended discussion of issues that have exercised human thought for centuries, but only to articulate some of these critical questions and make explicit my own—debatable—assumptions. This is necessary in order to make understandable the whole argument of the book and to invite a dialogue with other views and approaches.[3]

FACTS AND CONSCIOUSNESS

It would be possible to discuss the whole history of philosophy in terms of the relation between two sets of categories, those related to "reality" and those related to "consciousness." There are various ways of expressing these categories. Clovodis Boff has a list of them that begins with the following pairings:[4]

Pragmatism	PRAXIS	THEORY	Theoreticism
Determinism	WORLD	CONSCIOUSNESS	Utopianism
Positivism	FACTS	MEANING	Voluntarism
Objectivism	OBJECT	SUBJECT	Subjectivism
Empiricism	EXPERIENCE	TRUTH	Dogmatism
Realism	BEING	THOUGHT	Idealism

The relation between the pairs (here set in capital letters) can be established in a nondialectical way by emphasizing one member to the exclusion or minimization of the other. Such undialectical relations (as the table above tries to illustrate) can give us a number of conflicting philosophies (named in small letters at both ends of each line). When this happens we end up with an ethical theory that is quite barren. It is barren on the one hand because reality appears as a closed system—which accordingly makes human action meaningless—and on the other because thought closes on itself as an autonomous reality that excludes the world, in which case ethics remains at best mere explanation without efficacy.

The relation between these pairs, however, can also be established dialectically. Such a dialectical relation begins with a recognition at the analytical level of the primacy of praxis (and related categories): PRAXIS (and the terms beneath it) is the primary condition for the possibility of the paired term THEORY (and the terms beneath it). To this extent theory (the intervention of human thought, intention, and will in the human exchange with the world) becomes a function of praxis. But such intentionality—and to that extent theory, however elemental its form—is inherent in all human action. Praxis, and only human action can be called praxis, is indeed in itself already a dialectical concept involving both theory and action. It is dialectical also in a further sense, in that the two terms (theory and praxis) are not related to one another in a sort of stable equilibrium; such perfect harmonization could be produced only in the realm of thought, falling back on pure idealism in which dialectics would come to an end. On the contrary, instead of a balanced harmony we must think in terms of two poles that challenge each other, making change and movement possible. Action overflows and challenges the theory that has informed it; and thought, projecting the shape and future of reality, pushes action to new ventures. Reality is transformed through human action, and action is corrected and reoriented by reality. This dialectical interplay seems to be the necessary presupposition for political ethics.

We can illustrate and deepen this reflection by means of a brief

analysis of the problem of ethics in Marx. As Maximilien Rubel points
out, the interpretations of Marx have run in two opposite directions,
both building on statements of Marx himself.[5] At one extreme we have
those statements which seem to make human consciousness a mere
reflection of the economic process, which in turn is determined by
material laws. Thus, Marx quotes with approval an interpretation of his
thought by a Russian revolutionary: "He [Marx] envisages the social
movement as a natural chain of historical phenomena subject to laws
which are not only independent of the will, the conscience, and the
designs of men, but which on the contrary determine their will, their
conscience, and their designs."[6] No sooner are such statements quoted,
however—and there are hundreds of them—than other interpreters
confront us with equally strong statements underscoring human responsibility. It is not from the young "humanist" Marx but from the old
and ailing author of *Das Kapital* that we take this personal "witness" to
his convictions (in a letter dated April 30, 1867 to his friend S. Meyer):

> Why have I not answered you sooner? Because I have been constantly on
> the brink of death. As long as I was able to work, I therefore had to use
> every moment I could to finish my work, to which I have sacrificed my
> health, my joy of living, and my family. I trust that this explanation does
> not need any commentary. The so-called practical people make me laugh
> with their wisdom. If one would choose to be an animal, one could
> naturally turn his back on human suffering and busy himself in trying to
> save his own skin. But I would have considered myself very "unpractical" if
> I had died without at least having finished the manuscript of my book.[7]

These are not the words of a fatalist. They correspond to the sentence in
Marx's *The Holy Family:* "History does not do anything . . . rather it is
the living, real human being who does it all. . . . It is not history that uses
the human being as a means to fulfill its goals. . . . history is nothing but
human activity pursuing its own goals."

Is this merely a contradiction in Marx? If so, it is certainly not the
only one! Do we have to choose between material determinism and
human responsibility as most interpreters of Marx have done—either
by denying that a contradiction exists (a very difficult thing to do in
purely logical terms) or by explicitly rejecting or minimizing one of the
horns of the dilemma? Rubel, Sidney Hook, and a few others suggest
another possibility, which is best summarized in Hook's interpretation
of Marx's affirmation that "communism is inevitable":

> Communism is not destined to be realized by the nature of things; but, *if
> society is going to survive,* communism offers the only way out of the

impasse created by the inability of capitalism to provide a *decent social existence* to its salaried employees, and this in spite of the overabundance of wealth. The affirmation of Marx is really this: either this (communism) or nothing (barbarism). The objectivity of Marxism consists in the reality of this dilemma, its subjectivity in the fact that it chooses *this* rather than *nothing*. Normally, the recognition of the reality of the dilemma brings with it a commitment to communism. But this is in no way more *necessary* than the recognition that milk is a healthy beverage makes the drinking of milk necessary. . . . It is only when you choose the first term of the dilemma, which means that you perform a psychological and ethical act, that you have the right to call yourself a Marxist. . . . The objective truth of Marxism is fulfilled in the intelligent revolutionary act. Marxism is neither a science nor a myth; it is *a realistic method of social action.*[8]

We are not concerned here either with the intrinsic merit of Marx's own analysis or with the correctness of his statement of the dilemma. The important point is the nature of the ethical judgment and decision implied in this interpretation: the rigorous use of socioanalytical tools, applied both to history and to the present, points the direction in which a human future *can* be built and indicates the results of refusing that future. (For Marx, this possibility is communism, and its rejection means chaos and inhumanity; he claims that this dilemma is substantiated by objective analysis.) *But human beings have to decide.* Ethical options are posed by reality (which naturally includes previous human decisions and options). To dream of ethical decisions outside this framework of reality is the illusion of moralism. But history will not in any fatal or mechanistic way decide for men; the decision will always be a human decision.

In his early work, as he tried to develop a project of "religious socialism," Paul Tillich came close to this formulation of the ethical situation in his idea of the *kairos,* a historical opportunity that has to be seized.[9] The point in both cases is that such historical opportunities cannot be invented or imagined; they emerge—according to Marx in relation to "infrastructural" developments—and have to be "discerned" through the application of sociohistorical analysis. This, for Marx, is the difference between a "utopian" socialism and a "scientific" socialism.

Two other elements, however, are implied in such a position: (1) There is a previous commitment, which is expressed by Marx negatively: "If one would choose to be an animal. . . ." Marx decided to be "human," not "to turn his back on human suffering," to support "the dignity of the worker," to embrace the decision of the man who chooses to "create himself." Certainly Marx would claim that this is not an arbitrary commitment but a fulfillment demanded by the objective conditions. This, however, is something that cannot be proved empirically; it is not a fact but a claim that can be validated only in its realization. (2) Political praxis, therefore, becomes an essential part of the argument. It challenges present reality in the name of the future that is hidden in its womb, struggling to be born yet always in peril of being swallowed by the "dragon" (Rev. 12:1ff.).

The unstable, dialectical relation between facts and consciousness, theory and praxis now becomes clearer. Facts constitute the framework and support for decision. Theory is a human construction abstracted from past and present praxis that in turn opens the way for a new praxis. Praxis incorporates a theory and challenges it by changing the reality from which it has been abstracted.

Elsewhere I have suggested some reasons why, from a Christian perspective, it is necessary to question some of the assumptions in this interpretation.[10] But insofar as the relation between reality and consciousness, praxis and theory is concerned, we can use this perspective as a fruitful hypothesis for reflecting on a Christian ethics of politics.

THE QUESTION OF PERSPECTIVE

We spoke a moment ago about previous human decisions and options which point the way to our judgments and decisions. But such previous options are themselves partly conditioned by our "location" within social reality and they in turn condition our analysis. We cannot, therefore, avoid the question: Who are the Christians—or the Christian theologians—who confront this fact of political reflection and decision? Whence do they derive their knowledge? To whom are they accountable? What influences their method and the conditions of their work?

The response to this question must begin with the recognition of a "double location," as in the case of other scientists or thinkers: On the one hand there is the theologian's location within a theological discipline with its particular epistemological conditions and demands; on the other hand the theologian is also a social agent within a particular social formation.

The social sciences in general—particularly the sociology of knowledge—have rendered us acutely aware of this "second location" of the scientist within social reality. It is therefore important not to fall into the kind of sociological determinism that would regard the theological enterprise as merely reflective of a social location. In the case of theological reflection, the impact of social location has to be evaluated and thought through with reference to the particularity of theological knowledge. Theology is not a "sanctified sociology." It is a knowledge that has not only a specific form of apprehension, a specific epistemological principle—faith—and a fundamental reference (namely, God in his revelation in a special history that is fulfilled in Jesus Christ and made available and operative in history by the power of the Holy Spirit) but also an immediate social reference, that is, the Christian community.

[In Latin America, for example, we have found it necessary to relate our theology to a commitment to the struggle for liberation, a struggle that has a predominantly social and political dimension; we have therefore found it necessary to take very seriously a socioanalytical mediation for theological thinking. *But we intend to do theology,* not sociology or politics. Moreover, we believe that theological reflection, while it is related to the political praxis of Christians, is not a mere reflection of that praxis. It has its own *logos,* its own structure and identity as theology. We are not fanatics proposing spontaneous or pragmatic action or rhetorical thinking. We believe that the questions which emerge in the praxis of liberation must be articulated and dealt with within theology's sphere of competence and using the instruments of theological thinking.]

If we take seriously this matter of double location, we have to ask how its significance is to be evaluated. In particular, how can the meaning of the social location be assessed without voiding the specificity of the theological enterprise? There are at least three ways of posing this question: (1) A social location determines a perspective. It conceals some things and reveals others. We have sometimes referred to this in terms of "the epistemological privilege of the poor." The poor are not morally or spiritually superior to others, but they do see reality from a different angle or location—and therefore differently. (2) A social location poses questions that can be articulated as problems and themselves made the object of study. There is, for example, for any theoretical work the unavoidable question as to what is worthy of being thought *denkwürdige* (as Heidegger calls it): How do we choose the subjects? What is relevant (and consequently what is irrelevant and alienating) in the questions chosen to be addressed? (3) The destination of our work has to be considered: to what end is it related? No doubt there is a certain gratuitousness in all thinking worthy of the name (otherwise it becomes mere opportunism), but at the same time all the productions of human thought have a social impact and the theologian cannot remain indifferent to the question: for whom? There is no socially uncommitted theology.

For human beings, however, social location is a matter not merely of fate or circumstance, but also of option and decision. We are *situated* in reality, to be sure—historically, geographically, culturally, and most of all groupwise and classwise—but we can also *position* ourselves differently in relation to that situation. The ethical question, therefore, passes through the decision about one's own social position, with one's option, one's slant on reality, one's choice of relevant subject, with the goal of one's work. What an analysis of the situation puts before us is the question of *how* we choose in relation to the alternatives and challenges we confront. This is one of the key points where a Christian commitment helps to determine the outcome. I shall argue at the end of chapter 6 that an eschatological ethics of justice, which assumes solidarity with the poor as its historical mediation, is the basis for this commitment.[11] For the moment, anticipating that discussion, I shall simply set down the following criterion: *Theological and social location for the Christian are one, unified in the specific commitment to the poor.* This is the determining option with respect to both the use of socioanalytical tools and the perspective for theological reflection.

SOCIOLOGIES: WHICH AND HOW?

Once we establish the need to relate theological-ethical reflection to social analysis, we face the question: which kind of social analysis (for they are many and conflicting) and how are we to articulate the relation? I shall make some comments on both questions but in reverse order.

Negatively, we would like to rule out two common approaches to relating theology and social analysis. The first involves the substitution of theological categories for sociological categories. In the form of empiricism, it attempts to relate to social situations as if it could understand them through mere observation, without realizing that this supposed "immediacy" hides a mediation. We do not meet any situation *as it is;* our "direct observation," even our "experience" itself, involves seeing through the prism of a certain "construction of reality" (Berger) that derives from tradition, either from dominant ideologies or from simple personal prejudices. This is true in the case of much social action that is commonly defended as practical, personal, or "Samaritan-like" in the Christian response to need, yet in fact is unconsciously built on a functionalist sociology and a reformist historical project. A similar and equally inadmissible approach to substituting theological for social analysis takes the form of a theological purism which fears the contamination of secular categories (particularly those that have emerged in explicit opposition to Christianity) and therefore wants to develop specifically Christian answers to secular problems. This is true at least in part of the Roman Catholic "social doctrine of the Church." Both at the level of accounting for "what is happening" in a particular social problem and at the level of articulating a "Christian answer," such "Christian social doctrine" has to use human concepts and categories. It cannot therefore avoid incorporating certain philosophical and sociological concepts which are usually "smuggled" into the supposedly Christian doctrine and hence sacralized without being subjected to rigorous examination and criticism. The "social doctrine" of property is a clear case in point.[12]

Much more attractive than empiricism and purism, but also negative and inadequate, is the approach involving not the substitution of theological for sociological categories but the "coordinating," or "mixing," of sociological and theological categories, as in the search for "correspondences," or "analogies," between biblical and contemporary situations. Boff says such thinking characteristically expresses itself in the form "apropos of . . ." or "speaking of. . . ."[13] Attempts, for example, to construct a "Christian" understanding of revolution by applying directly to contemporary situations Jesus' attitude toward the Zealots—which we know has yielded radically divergent results for different scholars—illustrates the pitfalls of this approach. The method of "analogy" used by Karl Barth in *The Christian Community and the Civil Community,* which was pursued even more systematically by Roger Mehl in *Pour une éthique sociale chrétienne,* represents a more systematic and adequate form of correlation. However, unless these "analogies" are supported by deeper work in which the legitimate autonomy of both the socioanalytical and the theological disciplines is duly respected, they frequently result in an arbitrary mixture in which predetermined conclusions are buttressed by superficial and even purely terminological similarities. Such "correspondences" while they may be useful in terms of their suggestive force for homiletical and spiritual theology, cannot be justified as the basis for serious theoretical construction.

A positive response to our question seems to require the recognition of social analysis as a constitutive moment in theological reflection on politics. It is "constitutive" for theology because theology has no other way of "knowing" the realm of the political except through such analysis; theology has no direct access to the political subject matter. It is only a "moment" in theology, however, because the "subject matter" to be investigated has to be focused theologically, that is, seen as a theological problem in terms that are appropriate to the theological discipline. Involved here is what, in the terminology introduced into philosophy by Gaston Bachelard, might be called "an epistemological break."[14] A new principle of knowledge is introduced, without which there is no theology properly speaking, but which cannot be legitimized for use within the field of human sciences because it corresponds to a faith-commitment—that is, according to Boff, God as Creator, Redeemer, and Fulfiller of creation and history is intrinsically related to all reality—and therefore "everything can be theologized."

We have variously spoken of social sciences, socioanalytical tools, and social analysis as giving access to the knowledge of political reality. The question cannot be evaded: which social analysis? which tools? what are the criteria for choosing between different and conflicting social theories and analyses? Ever since Max Weber, discussion about the possibility of a value-free social science has raged with such frequency and intensity as to suggest that the question is by no means a purely objective one. Actually, the psychology and sociology of the social sciences (even among such functionalist sociologists as Robert K. Merton[15]) seem to have made clear that there is no such thing as value-free science, least of all so far as the social sciences are concerned.

Naturally, in responding to this question we shall use the accepted criteria for evaluating scientific hypotheses and explanations—the ability to encompass the widest possible range of data and the ability to give a coherent and verifiable account of the phenomena. But this will take us only part of the way. With respect to the social sciences in particular, we will be forced to choose between two main streams which, even though including many variations and mixing their waters here and there, represent two radically different understandings of society. We refer to what can broadly be called the functionalist stream and the dialectical stream.[16] In a very broad sense—and at the risk of oversimplification—we can say that functionalist sociologies conceive of society as an organism, with social groups, classes, and functions being constitutive parts of that organism which should function harmoniously; conflicts are therefore understood as maladjustment and, directly or indirectly, social analysis serves the end of conflict solving.[17] Dialectical sociologies, on the other hand, have a conflictual understanding of society; viewing society as a complex phenomenon full of contradictions and conflicts, they undertake to understand the structural basis and dynamics of such conflicts.

It is our contention that these two divergent perspectives have their roots in two specific locations in social reality. The functionalist perspective is a vision "from the top," from the situation of those sectors of society (whether groups, classes, or nations) which exercise power and control and which therefore perceive society as basically a satisfactory organic system that must be preserved and perfected. Dialectical sociologies, on the other hand, express a vision "from below," from those sectors to which society appears as inadequate, badly structured, full of conflict, and in need of transformation. If this observation is correct, at least in its fundamental outlines, I would claim that the Christian is not without orientation for the choice that must be made.

This is why, without absolutizing or giving theological legitimation to its content, we have opted in principle for a dialectical as over against a functionalist social science. The dialectical approach corresponds more adequately to the perspective, the understandings, and the concerns that emerge in an option for solidarity with the poor. I have qualified this option because there are metaethical and metascientific questions with respect to the dialectical sociologies—as also with respect to the functionalist sociologies—that will have to be discussed. I refer, obviously, to their ideological and philosophical presuppositions. But then no scientific instrument—least of all in relation to the human—is free from such suppositions. This is why a critical attitude is essential. But such a critical attitude should not deter us from faithful and serious use of these instruments, or lead us to so-called neutral or unbiased attitudes that are in fact an illusion and usually end up by supporting the status quo.

SOCIAL PRAXIS AND
CHRISTIAN THEOLOGY

How can theology, without losing its integrity, incorporate this socioanalytical moment that we have regarded as constitutive? As a matter of fact, the issue is more complex than that, because we have to deal here with two distinct planes that constantly intersect. There is first the plane of praxis, to which we have assigned a certain priority; it includes political praxis in general and specifically the political praxis of Christians. Second, there is the plane of theory; this includes also general political theory and specifically Christian reflection on politics. Boff offers a diagram (p. 48) which I have found particularly illuminating for discussion of these complex relations.[18] We can immediately visualize several points: (1) There are two related planes or levels: at the level of praxis, A (political praxis in general) and A' (political praxis of Christians) belong in the same basic category; Christians do not have a "distinctive" politics. Specifically, in our case, we are speaking of the same historical project of liberation. This is why

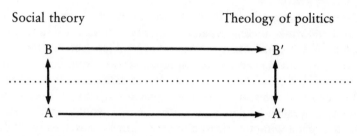

Social theory   Theology of politics

Political praxis   Political praxis of Christians

we have used the same symbol to characterize both, seeing Christian praxis (A′) as a form of the general political praxis (A) or—to put it in slightly different words—as the same political praxis qualified by the fact of being performed by a Christian. (2) A similar thing happens at the level of theory: the subject matter in both cases is again the same; theory is applied to the same problems and through use of the same analytical tools.[19] (3) Here too, however, at the level of theory, there is again a difference in agency. There is first a general "human" auspices, in which Christian commitment and perspective cannot be presupposed, and then there is a Christian auspices, the specificity of which lies precisely in these presuppositions. A correct understanding of the task of a theological ethics of politics demands that we keep these distinctions clearly in mind.

On the basis of this diagram, certain relations become immediately apparent: The vertical connection A↔B and A′↔B′ show the normal dialectical pairings so far as the relation between praxis and theory is concerned. We have already referred to the unity and difference between A and A′ and B and B′. But it is when we move beyond these self-evident relations that we come to the heart of the matter. The two major dangers—both theoretically and practically—appear in the diagonal connections.

The B′→A relation represents the attempt to build a theology of politics on the basis of secular political praxis alone, unrelated to the praxis of Christians. It is a tempting possibility, sometimes defended on the basis of a Christian kenosis that would relinquish Christian identity in order to achieve a "perfect incarnation" in the political realm. The result can only be a "secular," "death of God" theology. What happens is that A attracts B′ to its own sphere and theology ends up being mere social theory—and a bad one at that inasmuch as it becomes "an ideology that substitutes itself for an authentic social science" (Boff).

The A′→B relation is no less deceptive. A purely secular social theory cannot, for Christians, take the place of a theological ethics of politics, because it cannot account for the peculiar perspective of faith. The result is that Christians committed to the political struggle lack an adequate understanding of what they are doing, an understanding that could make sense for their faith; they end up living a dual existence in which their faith is neither enriched nor deepened by their praxis (thus resulting in an alienated faith) and their praxis is neither illumined nor qualified by their faith (thus diminishing the contribution that, as Christians, they owe to the common cause).

Political ethics is not a "game." It involves wrestling with the hard facts of political experience. The result of misguided attempts such as those suggested by the B'→A and A'→B diagonals is that, on the one hand, the "theologians" are isolated from the community of faith because they make theological claims that carry no weight since there is no "praxis substance" to them, and on the other hand Christians are confused and disoriented, their faith being unable to energize their praxis.

There are two fruitful approaches. These can be described in terms of connections signified in the diagram. The A→A'→B' connection suggests that Christian reflection on political praxis can be mediated by the experience of Christians engaged in political action. Here A' constitutes a first and indispensable hermeneutical key, the discernment of Christian faith and love, which acts out its obedience by assuming a historical praxis that is then subject to critical reflection on the basis of Scripture and Christian tradition.

The A→B→B' connection suggests that Christian reflection on political praxis can be mediated by secular social theory. Here B represents an equally necessary scientific key, the theoretical elaboration of a political praxis that is again assumed and then subjected to critical reflection from the standpoint of specifically Christian faith.

THEORETICAL MODELS

In its attempts to grasp "reality" human thought is forced to proceed by way of elaborating theoretical "models." These models are no more than "constructions of reality," never to be confused with reality as such, but to the extent that they abstract carefully and responsibly from praxis and experience they are necessary constructs, fruitful for advancing our knowledge of and our ability to shape the world. For our present purposes I would like to indicate some of the models we shall be using in our attempt to reflect on political ethics.

1. The French philosopher Paul Ricoeur worked out a structuralist

model which Enrique Dussel has applied to Latin American church history.[20] It distinguishes within a "civilization" (taking the word in a broad sense to include the totality of human construction, for example, "the Indian civilization" or "Western civilization") three layers (*paliers* is the word used by Ricoeur).

The first layer is that of the "tools" or "instruments" (*outils*) that the human being devises, invents, or creates in order to fulfill its purposes. The term includes the "tool," properly so-called from the stone ax to the computer, but it also embraces technology generally and the science on which technology feeds. This level is, on the whole, cumulative and transmissible; that is, it grows and is perfected and can be transposed from one civilization to another.

The second layer in the Ricoeur model corresponds to the "ethos" of a civilization, the complex of habits, attitudes, and relations that characterize it—for instance, the forms of relating to culture, to the past, and to nature, the attitudes toward work. These are characteristic of a civilization and are not easily transmissible. A change in the ethos of a civilization signifies a real "conversion" and deeply affects the institutions (social, political, religious) that both embody and support that ethos.

Finally, we have what Ricoeur calls the "core" (*Kern*)—Dussel calls it the "ethico-mythical nucleus"—of a civilization, its self-understanding, the way in which it interprets its origin and destiny, usually expressed in symbolic terms. Without this core, a civilization can have no unity or integrity.

2. This pattern of analysis is in many ways illuminating when we try to understand the relation of religion to a civilization. But it leaves unanswered a number of questions: How are these "layers" interrelated? By what mechanism do they reciprocally influence and determine one another? And above all, can this structuralist, synchronic model render a correct account of the uniqueness of particular social structures or the singularity of historical change? It is because of these unanswered questions that I like, side by side with this approach, to include the concepts of social formation and historical block which, as will immediately be apparent, have been developed in Marxist analysis.

The idea of social formation goes back to Marx himself. It designates a historically and geographically circumscribed society (such as Elizabethan England or czarist Russia) that is characterized by a more or less integrated and homogeneous economic system, political organization, and ideological perspective. According to Nicos Poulantzas, a modern Marxist theoretician, such a formation is "neither a whole where each of the elements is equivalent to the others as the phenomenon of an essence (as in Hegelianism), nor are any of those elements merely an epiphenomenon of one of them (as in economistic or mechanistic interpretations); the elements are asymmetrically related but autonomous; one of them is dominant."[21] We need not go along with Poulantzas in regarding the economic factor as "in the final analysis the determining one," the element that determines which of the others may be immediately dominant in any given social formation. His concept, however, includes a number of interesting features: (1) There is a recognition of the existence and relative autonomy in any particular social formation of several elements—the economic, the political, the ideological, the religious. (2) There is the insight that the importance of and the relation between these elements is not the same in each social formation. (3) There is the implicit recognition that each of the elements conditions the others, none being independent. (4) There is the observation that in a particular social formation one of these elements may play a dominant role; according to Marx, for instance, in the feudal social formation the ideological factor—in the form of religion—had this dominant role, while in the capitalist formation the economic factor has assumed that place. (5) Finally, there is the warning that no particular social formation corresponds absolutely to one mode of production (ancient, feudal, or capitalist) but that there is almost always an overlapping that involves more than just one such mode.

3. The idea of historical block was developed by the slightly "heretical" Marxist Antonio Gramsci. It corrects this exclusively sociological approach with a historical one: At a particular point in history, a social formation has a unity which is an "ensemble" in which theory and praxis, science and structure cohere and are expressed in an ideology. One could say that the material forces constitute the content while the ideology constitutes the form, or—in Gramsci's own metaphor—that "ideology serves to cement and to unify."[22] That ideology in turn is the ideology of whatever particular social class at any given historical juncture is dominant in the particular social formation. And this is what gives unity and distinctiveness to any given historical block.

4. Naturally, this leads to a fourth category—ideology. Since ideology is a much debated concept, I shall at this point limit myself simply to a working definition of the way in which I intend to use the term. For our purposes here an ideology is "a system (possessing its own internal logic and rigor) of representations (images, myths, ideas, concepts) which have an existence and a historic role in a given society."[23] In this rather formal definition I do not distinguish between ideology in a

negative sense (as hiding reality) and ideology in a positive sense (as a mobilizing force) nor do I distinguish between an unconscious and a conscious ideology. I would stress only two points: (a) An ideology does not "float in the air" but is related to the real existence of social groups and classes which at the same time condition and are conditioned by the ideology. (b) An ideology expresses at the level of representations (and therefore not necessarily in a rational way) relations that are actually lived out in society.

5. Finally, I would like to introduce a concept that appears frequently in Latin American sociological and theological literature, the idea of historical project. This concept has to do with models for the future. A vision of the future may take the form of a "utopia" (a concept with which we shall deal more fully in chapters 4 and 7). The utopian vision does not necessarily define coherent structures, much less the process through which they can be attained. It has no *topos,* no location in the sense of historical mediation and articulation. At the other extreme, the concern for the future may take the form of plans and programs which—given the diversity of goals—determine the means, time schedules, strategies, and tactics. The idea of historical project finds its place somewhere between these two extremes. It is a vision of the future that is sufficiently precise in its political, social, and economic contours as to constitute a coherent goal that can be expected to be realized in history. While there is still great flexibility in detail with respect to defining the model to be pursued and determining the technical means for achieving it, the historical project is sufficiently concrete to provide a guide for action and to elicit commitment. We could thus speak of American expansionism overseas, Mahan's theory of naval supremacy, the New Deal, or Kennedy's developmentalism as historical projects.

It is interesting to introduce here a distinction that will become illuminating later when we deal in the next two chapters with the Latin American situation. The distinction is drawn by Hugo Assmann:

> I would distinguish two levels of historical projects: one in which, while maintaining the priority of the political, the lines of technical projections are nevertheless visible, albeit only partially, in a rather symbolic-allusive form, through partial identifications; and a second one in which a technical model is first of all defined in both its entirety and its details, to the detriment of the political line.[24]

This whole discussion of categories and models may seem rather technical and uninspiring. After all, the theologian, as theologian, is not a prophet. The pronouncements of the prophets are synthetic, while the task of the theologian is analytic. God created his prophetic "congregation" of the end-time for announcing and enacting within historical time the coming of his kingdom. The theologian serves the prophetic ministry of the church. Theologians have preliminary work to do as preparation for that ministry; they are also on the scene afterward to reflect critically on what has been done. But they should not try to substitute themselves for that prophetic ministry of the church. In this chapter we have simply tried to lay some analytical groundwork in order that we might introduce a specific historical "case"—that of Latin America. The Latin American experience may prove helpful in our endeavor to elaborate an approach to a theological political ethics.

4

Latin America: From Authoritarianism to Democracy

In a profound and fascinating study of political ethics, Paul Lehmann writes: "The responsibility for the *determination* of priorities is a *theological* one. The responsibility for the *identification* of the priorities is a *historical* one."[1] There is, as we have tried to point out, a dialectical relation between the two. If our methodological presuppositions are correct, we should begin with the "historical identification." This we intend to do on the basis of a concrete historical situation, namely Latin America. The reason for this choice is obvious: Latin America is the specific location of my own praxis and reflection. But if our understanding of this specific situation is sufficiently profound, it should yield results that are relevant for other conditions and locations. Besides, by reason of its peculiar geographic and historical situation Latin America is a remarkably faithful mirror and thermometer of the dilemmas and crises of both the underdeveloped and the developed worlds, one that can bring into sharp focus a picture of the social-economic-political system of the entire world.

We would like here to explore particularly the role of religion and Christianity in shaping, supporting, and challenging the various historical projects in Latin American history. There is a reason for my choosing this approach: we are witnessing in our day, everywhere in the world, a revival of the symbiosis between religion and politics. The Muslim revolutions, the massive involvement of conservative evangelicals in the recent political life of the U.S., the religious claims of military governments and the political concern of "base communities" in Latin America, as well as the denunciation of political oppression on the part of the church, and the religious roots and overtones of the peace movements—all witness in their various and frequently conflicting ways to the fact that the age-old connection between religion and politics has by no means disappeared from our so-called secularized world.

This observation about world developments in general also points to more particular reason for my focusing on Latin America: the decisive moments in the social history of Latin America are characterized in many ways and to a greater or lesser degree by the presence of an important religious dimension or component. This is evident not only in our colonial history, shaped as it was by the symbiotic relationship between the Iberian ethos and the Catholic Church, but also in the struggles for independence and modernization and in the various conflictive political projects afoot today on the subcontinent. This fact gives to the process of secularization in our Latin American situation a distinctive character: those features which rightly or wrongly (we suspect wrongly) are considered typical in the Northern Hemisphere—the end of ideologies, functional thinking, the "death of god"—are present in Latin America only among small elites. Is this simply a matter of cultural lag, a delay that will eventually be overcome? Or does it have to do rather with our wholly different form of historical development? Whatever the interpretation, Latin America is not a secularized continent in which religion plays only a marginal role. In other words, a consideration of the religious factor in political decisions—and here, as Weber teaches us, is where our theological-ethical inquiry should begin—must be part of any adequate analysis of the past, present, and future in Latin America.

THE HISTORICAL RESIDUE
OF ABORTED UTOPIAS

Orlando Fals-Borda, a Colombian sociologist, has observed with respect to the history of his country (and the experience has been universal throughout Latin America) that "utopian ideas are found at the beginning of each of the great periods of transition" and that after the social process has run its course "the utopia has been conditioned and only its historical residue is left."[2] This is particularly true for the first such period, the creation of the colonial order. At the time of the conquest of America, Spain was at the zenith of its power and glory— besides being well advanced on its road toward economic decadence. The flourishing of its art and literature, its proud spirit of independence, the recovery and unification of its territory, its dream of creating a "Christian kingdom" overseas—all were the last ephemeral flowerings of the feudal medieval order, planted in the soil of a "poor and backward" economy[3] which could operate only as "a middleman, handling raw materials and finished goods like a merchant and leaving the larger profits to the industrialized nations."[4] The colonial order in Latin America bears the marks of this contradiction.

The discovery of America was interpreted from the beginning in religious terms. Enrique Dussel has expressed it poignantly: "In Spain there existed, therefore, something akin to a 'temporal messianism' in which the destiny of the nation and the destiny of the Church were believed to be united. Hispanic Christianity, it was believed, was unique in that the nation had been elected by God to be the instrument for the salvation of the world. This idea among the Spanish that they had been elected by God . . . constituted the foundation of the religio-politics of Isabel, Charles, and Philip."[5] This is the "absolute utopia" (Fals-Borda). The seriousness with which it was assumed is attested by the theological discussions about the "legitimate right" of conquest, the Spanish king's "just title" to the new lands, and the "human nature" of the Indians. The idealistic "laws of the Indies" are the magna charta of that utopia, the attempt to legislate the humanistic vision of the most advanced theologians (such as Vitoria) into a just and Christian society. Behind and below this utopia, though, a historical project was taking shape, the "transmission and reproduction of an ideology with additions, substitutions, and adaptations; that is, of the seigniorial society that prevailed on the Iberian peninsula."[6]

It has been hotly debated whether the Spanish conquest should be seen as a feudal or a capitalist enterprise. Economically, Spain was mercantilist; it conceived its relation to the new colonies in term of "trade," the exchange of their raw materials, agricultural products, and gold and silver for its own manufactured goods. Since Spain was such a poor producer of manufactured goods, however, the Spanish monopoly on the Latin American economy did not result in a capitalization of either Spain or America; on the contrary the capital generated through trade ended in the capitalist nations of the north. Thus, without itself being an industrialized capitalist nation, Spain introduced Latin America into the industrial-capitalist "circuit." The second element in this historical project was the reproduction within the colonies of a caste society, a social formation characterized by a rigid caste system that was justified by ideological religion (and theology) as a law of creation.

The economic system and the caste structure were given permanence in the so-called *ley indiana,* that is, in the Spanish institutions as they really came to function in America—the Spanish feudal system of the *behetria* developed as the American *encomienda,* a form of forced labor; the Spanish sheep-raising *mesta* organized in America as the *hacienda,* the large cattle farm of the land baron.[7]

In such seigniorial social formation the role of religion is important. Religion establishes the permanence of the order. It acts as a "cement."

It sanctions the institutions, values, and norms and transmits the myths and symbols through which reality is apprehended—nature, interrelationships, the meaning of life.

Specifically, in the colonial order, we can identify two such functions of religion: (1) The religious utopia of the "Christian kingdom" sacralized the colonial enterprise—the point has been amply documented and need not detain us here. (2) Religion was also one of the most important instruments of domination. The characteristics of the early conquest have in this respect been decisive: what happened in America was not an encounter of two cultures, the kind of encounter that could—and in some cases did—produce an inner transformation of the "ethico-mythical nucleus" or core of one of the two cultures. On the contrary, what was involved here was a tabula rasa policy that totally dislodged the Indian culture by eliminating its leaders, destroying its institutions, and subverting its economic infrastructure: the ethico-mythical core of the invading Christian culture was imposed. Certainly the Indians transformed, adapted, and interpreted the new religion. But their former identity as peoples was disrupted beyond recovery. Together with the physical conquest, a kind of spiritual "genocide" had also taken place. The new religion was imposed—and in a peculiar way accepted. But it was the religion of the conqueror, a permanent sign of defeat.

Fals-Borda describes this process in terms of the substitution of values: (1) The indigenous values of animism, nature, and family easily coalesced with Spanish religious beliefs and practices to produce the "folk Catholicism" that persists in much of Latin America today. (2) The Spanish-Christian value of otherworldliness, however, became a substitute for an indigenous "futurism." The Indians "took refuge in otherworldliness as an escape from subjugation; their boredom with this world was sublimated in visions of the otherworld that were presented to them by the indoctrinating priests."[8] (3) Finally, the value of Manichaeism (by which Fals-Borda means the idea that human nature, especially as regards its physical existence, is sinful), which was contrary to the moral experience of the Indian but constituted the necessary presupposition for a prescriptive morality, generated the "simulation" and "reserve" that whites were later fond of referring to as "the hypocrisy of the Indian."

Perhaps nothing more movingly expresses this fact of religious domination than the images of Christ in Indian and mestizo art in the seventeenth and eighteenth centuries. There was the "suffering Christ," the image of defeat and impotence, the defeated Christ in whom the Indians find their own identity, and there was the "exalted Christ," the conqueror, the heavenly king, the image of the "divinized Spanish conqueror" who decides the destiny of the Indian and to whom the Indian has no direct access, who must be propitiated and placated.[9]

On the whole, therefore, we can characterize religion in the colonial society as a "political religion" (within the limitations that have always characterized Christianity in this respect)—the religious underpinning of society and its structures. This is what the nineteenth-century revolutionaries came to denounce as "the unholy alliance of throne and altar." Such a conclusion, however, would be one-sided, for it was precisely within this established Christendom that prophetic criticism made itself heard. Religion, in colonial Latin America, to use the typology of Desroche,[10] fulfilled the function not only of "legitimation" or integration (*attestation*), but also of "protest within"[11] (*contestation*) and even of radical protest (*protestation*). I need only refer here to the efforts of the religious orders (particularly the Jesuits) to distinguish the church from the Spanish administration, and Christianity from the religion of the Spanish *señores,* and to the efforts of many bishops to "order" the life of the church to the benefit of the Indians, and the prophetic-pastoral voices raised to plead the cause of the Indian.[12] Indeed it is impossible not to pause here to recall the long list of martyrs stretching from Bishop Antonio Valdivieso of Nicaragua who was murdered in 1550 by a captain and a group of soldiers because (as a contemporary chronicle puts it), while "preaching in favor of the freedom of the Indians, he reproved the conquistadores and governors," to Archbishop Oscar Arnulfo Romero of El Salvador who was murdered in 1980 by the same people for the same reason!

THE STRUGGLE FOR FREEDOM:
FOR WHOM AND FOR WHAT?

The eighteenth century witnessed the decay of the Spanish Empire, the nineteenth century its collapse. Most Latin American countries became independent between 1810 and 1850, as the British Empire wrested control of the seas from Spain and claimed for its own industrial-capitalist expansion the resources and markets of the Iberian colonies. The colonial aristocracy—landowners and mine owners, children of the conquistadores—were quick to discern "the signs of the times" and latch onto the new modern world being inaugurated by the Anglo-Saxon nations. British free-trade economics, French revolutionary ideology (in a variety of ways and to varying degrees), and the North American revolution provided the ideology and the models.

The real import of the change became apparent, however, only during the second and third quarters of the nineteenth century when conservatives and liberals struggled for the power to shape the new nations. Eventually, the liberals prevailed in most Latin American countries and by the last quarter of the nineteenth century a definite historical project was afoot in Latin America. The economic and political features of this project have been carefully researched and expounded. Its feasibility rested on what is usually called the neocolonial pact—a community of interests established between the Latin American elites and various European (mainly British) and American (U.S.) interests based on the exchange of raw materials (and eventually some semifactured goods) for manufactured goods and services. The intent of these elites—involving a continuing mix of utopian and ideological elements—was the modernization of the countries and the establishment of modern democratic republics (witness the constitutions of most Latin American states). To populate, to educate, to stimulate initiative, and to ensure freedom—these were the goals defined by the "bourgeois" elites that governed the most important Latin American countries since the end of the nineteenth century.

But their intention was even more encompassing. Dussel (who cannot be suspected of any great sympathy for these elites) has evaluated their achievement:

> At the level of *civilization,* the Latin American nations began to feel the enormous Anglo-Saxon impact from Great Britain and North America, an impact which was in reality neocolonialist with its commerce, technology, and schools of engineering. On the level of *culture* and of the *mythical-nucleus,* liberalism for the first time made an impact on the opinion of the political-cultural elite. This resulted in a veritable transformation of the elements of the collective Latin American consciousness, first at the level of the institutions and subsequently among the populace as a whole. A pluralistic society, a secular civilization developed in Latin America and is a twentieth-century fact—especially in the large cities, the universities, the labor unions, and among the ruling minorities.[13]

Roman Catholicism perceived this change as a threat and, in keeping with European ultramontanism, took its stand against it—on the whole unsuccessfully. The effort was unsuccessful because, apart from a few exceptions, it could not at the time (due to a number of historical circumstances) command the intellectual strength to come to terms with this challenge, and so experienced the same fluctuating fortunes as the defeated conservatives. It is interesting, therefore, to pause for a moment and look at the role played at this juncture of history by Protestantism. We shall attempt only a sketch of the developments.

THE FAITH FOR A NEW DAY

Two conditions facilitated the introduction of Protestantism into Latin America. Externally there was the neocolonial pact which favored the development of relationships with the northern—Protestant—countries. Internally there was the victory of the modernizing elites over the traditional elites. At this point we will consider only the latter, the internal condition.

The modernizing, or liberal, elites rightly regarded the Roman Catholic Church as a basic obstacle in the path of progress toward modernity. They regarded Protestantism as an ally in their own cause, partly because they perceived it as the religion of freedom, individualism, private judgment, education, and personal morality. These elites did not themselves become Protestant, but they did open up the doors of the new countries, and sometimes specifically invited and sought to attract Protestant immigrants and missions.

Protestant proclamation in Latin America emphasized above all the call to personal conversion—in keeping with the theology and praxis of the Anglo-American "evangelical awakenings." In comparison with Roman Catholic form and ritual, Protestant preaching stressed the need for personal encounter with Jesus Christ, a vivid experience of forgiveness and a new moral life. The convert understood himself as "a new man." Personal testimonies repeatedly use such expressions: "I became a different person"; "I was like a newborn baby"; "I began a new life."

On closer examination, we see in the impact of this process clear signs of the transition from a traditional to a modern society, from the feudal to the bourgeois person. Three features of the transition stand out.

The first feature is that of individualism. Persons are invited to become individually different, distinctive, to make a decision that is exclusively their own, one that uproots them from the structures to which they naturally belong, such as their family and circle of friends. Again the personal testimonies commonly attest to this: I "leave my friends" or "break with my family." True, such converts enter a community, but it is a voluntaristic community, built on the basis of independent individual decisions. Preaching emphasizes the elimination of all "social mediations": "you stand alone before Christ"; "you have to decide for yourself." Eternal life and eternal death hang on the outcome of this moment of decision. In a way, immigrants or peasants who have migrated to the city—anonymous members of the new subproletariat—are thus challenged, perhaps for the first time, to take in hand their own destiny. Clearly we find ourselves here in the world of the "free individual" of modern society.

The second element in this transition of which we speak is that of subjectivity. In the more traditional religion to which Latin Americans were accustomed, religious categories are projected on a supernatural screen. Natural processes such as rainfall and sickness are subordinate to supernatural causes or decisions—saints, spirits, demons, various suprahuman powers. Religious actions or observances are designed to affect—either more or less magically as the case may be—this supernatural realm and to win its favor. The supernatural, of course, does not disappear in Protestant teaching (though it is limited to God and the devil), but its operation is perceived and portrayed in a different way: it is projected on the screen of subjectivity. Again, the personal testimonies utilize such key words as "peace," "certainty," "joy," "experience." The cosmic struggle of the powers has been transposed to the sphere of personal consciousness. Clearly we find ourselves here— within the religious sphere—in a Cartesian world.

Finally, as has been underscored so often, religious conversion involves a transition also in the moral realm. The focus now is on internalization of duty, a sense of responsibility, and the virtues of early capitalism—industry, honesty, moderation, frugality. Here is the universe of moral achievement, of self-improvement. Once again, in religious and moral terms we find ourselves in the world of Immanuel Kant. We are now fully aware of the social impact of those moral virtues.

With respect to these three features, in short, we can say that "the new creature," when it takes concrete psycho-social-ethical form, manifests the personal features of the bourgeois world rather than those of traditional society. In limited numbers within a limited sector, Protestantism helps to create persons who correspond to and contribute to the change in social structure and mentality. It reinforces the liberal bourgeois utopia of the free moral agent.

The emphasis on personal conversion was also related in Latin America to a radical—sometimes virulent—polemics against Roman Catholicism. Polemicists drew upon the whole arsenal of arguments developed in Europe from the time of the Reformation to the First Vatican Council. Protestant polemics (or perhaps anti-Roman eristics) in Latin America tended to follow—and interrelate—three lines of argument, all of which, from their own perspectives, share a common aim.

The first of the three, and perhaps the central one, has been summarized by W. Stanley Rycroft in terms of the faith/religion antithesis.[14] "Religion" is interpreted here—at its worst, of course—as idolatry, superstition, a semipaganism hidden behind formal worship and dogmas that remain external to the life of the people; behind this negative image lies an even more fundamental motif—a rejection of religion as something transmitted and inherited with culture and mediated by institutions, sacrament, and priesthood. Protestantism by the same token is seen in this scheme as a "living religion," or "faith," and conversion accordingly means liberation from a socioreligious structure as well as an opening to subjectivity.

A second polemical line takes up the classical arguments against such things as papacy, tradition, and mediation of the Virgin and saints. But it is interesting to notice that discussion of these doctrinal questions centers no longer in the classical theological arguments (though they are still cited) but in an attempt to show that "Rome" uses false doctrine in order to "enslave," to "keep in ignorance," and to "dominate the conscience" of the people.

This observation leads us to the third, and in many ways most typical, line of argument—the sociocultural polemics. Catholicism is seen as cause, bearer, and consequence of the feudal period, those Dark Ages that are synonymous with social and political oppression, scholastic obscurantism, ignorance, and cultural lag. All the Protestant congresses from Panama (1916) to Buenos Aires (1949) sound this note. Catholicism is considered the ideology and religious structure of a total system, that of the outworn seigniorial Hispanic order that was forced on Latin America and must now disappear in order to make way for a new democratic order of freedom. Protestantism, which has historically inspired such order, offers itself as a religious alternative for the new world.

Having looked at Protestantism from the perspective of the modernizing elites within Latin America, we may now look at the complementary side of the picture—the origins, motivations, and historical context of the "sending" agent, namely the British and American missionary enterprise. There is a complex relation between the Protestant missionary enterprise and the expansion of the northern capitalist world, which we cannot go into at this point. What is clear though, in relation to Latin America, is that Protestantism claimed and (within its limitations) assumed the role that the Latin American liberal elites had assigned it in the transition from a traditional society to the modern bourgeois world.

Protestantism of course assesses this new order in different ways, but in alliance with liberals—and particularly with Freemasons—it fights for religious freedom and various aspects of secularization (cemeteries, schools) that it sees to be needed for its own life and expansion. In their educational services, some of the churches attempt to provide for the formation of enlightened liberal elites. But Protestantism's most important service to the new society is to offer to some people in the uprooted masses a new life style, a new self-understanding, a religion that enables them to live in the new world now opening up. At the level of ethos and nucleus (or core, to use the terminology of Ricoeur's model) Protestantism participates in the subversion of the old order and the creation of the new.

When the Latin American Missionary Congress met in Montevideo in 1926, optimism was running high. Such great missionary leaders as John A. Mackay, Robert E. Speer, and Samuel Guy Inman looked with joy on the new Latin America just being born—to which Protestantism was making and would make a decisive contribution. Theirs was not the condescending or imperialistic mentality of American expansionism. Theirs was rather a genuine enthusiasm for this new world—being born of the encounter between the modern world and the Latin spirit under the dynamic influence of the Christian gospel. Inman envisioned "a stable political life, a strong middle class as a balance wheel, a readjustment of the old social order to new democratic forms . . . the founding of a proper moral and spiritual basis to assure permanence in national life."[15] Robert Speer confidently identifies his own view with that of the Montevideo meeting that articulated so well the optimistic mood of North and South American Protestant leadership—and in turn reflected the high hopes of the whole modernizing project:

> In almost all South American countries since 1916 have occurred events and developments tending to enhance the significance and to accentuate the need of evangelical ideals. There have been signal suggestions, if not of the direct impact of these ideals, at least of an environment increasingly hospitable to their application. There have been revivals of religious interest, intellectual and educational awakenings, reassertions of independence and individuality in the pursuit of truth, a heightened emphasis on moral values, crusades against vice, ignorance, and injustice, upsurgings of altruistic sentiment organized into reforming philanthropies, economic readjustments, and commerical expansion conceived in terms of common welfare, manifestations of national and international good will touching a new world order. A new wave of constructive social idealism [Inman did not hesitate to speak of "social democracy"], sane, modernistic, spiritual, and resolute in its trend, has moved upon the minds of alert leaders in both the Andean and the Atlantic republics. It has been humanitarian and practical rather than political and dogmatic—unlike the doctrinaire dreamings, the aristocratic ideologies, the ecclesiastical manifestoes which often, in the past, have soared above the people and ignored the deeper problems of progressive democracies.

So fervent, in some of the countries, have been the new aspirations, so
radical the insurgencies against obscurantism and tradition, so clear the
demand for a renovated social order, that observant students mark a fresh,
creative outburst of the Latin American spirit. Some writers hail the new
day as a renaissance.[16]

The date was 1926, and Protestants believed in and worked for "the
new renaissance" in Latin America.

5

Latin America: From Democracy to the National Security State

The news coming out of Latin America the last few years—news of social unrest, guerrilla activity escalating in some cases to civil war, military coups, repressive governments, systematic violations of human rights, economic crises—cannot but prompt the question: whatever happened to the project for democratic modernization? whatever became of the bright and prosperous future on which Protestant churches throughout the world and the liberal elites in Latin America had—if I may be permitted the expression—bet so heavily? We sowed modern democracy and reaped the national security state. What went wrong?

As we address this question we will not attempt a detailed history of the developments. Our concern is rather to sketch a specific background for answering the question about ethical commitment in politics. In other words, we want to illustrate in concrete form the assertion we made in the words of Paul Lehmann: "The responsibility for the identification of the priorities is a *historical* one." How is it possible to discern the direction in which a human future can be built—and the results of refusing that future?

THE INVISIBLE COUNTRY
BECOMES VISIBLE

In order to do this we must begin with a brief historical account starting roughly in the second and third decades of our century, when what one Argentine bishop called "the invisible country" became visible. Up to this point, Latin American history had been the history of its elites. The "people"—the Indians, mixed bloods, peasants, Afro-Americans—had been "the absent ones," passive objects, silent sufferers, the "human commodity" transferred from the colonial to the neocolonial pact.

Several factors conspired to make the invisible visible. The economic crisis of the capitalist West in 1929, coming shortly after World War I, marked a critical juncture for the neocolonial pact. In the space thereby opened up, some national oligarchies began to develop their own industrial projects, displacing certain imports by processing at home certain raw materials, while immigration and natural growth led to population increase. Around all this new industry, state administration, and commerce a limited but significant *petite bourgeoisie* began to develop. More important, in the cities and in some rural areas an urban proletariat and subproletariat emerged; in some countries they organized. This modernizing project, given the international economic and political conditions at the beginning of the thirties, resulted in the unexpected emergence of a mass society.

The more enlightened members of the liberal elite soon realized the importance of this new situation. As early as the twenties a few of them, convinced by the socialist ideas coming out of Europe and motivated in many cases by strong moral idealism, began in their own countries to form socialist and communist groups and parties, which usually enlisted very few members—from the *petite bourgeoisie* and the more advanced proletariat. More widespread, however, was the attempt to develop "populist" nationalist movements, bringing together the progressive national oligarchies and the people.

The Peruvian Popular Party (APRA—Alianza Popular Revolucionaria Americana) was the first and perhaps most visible expression of this development. Its program included several main objectives: opposition to American imperialism; the political unity of Latin America; progressive nationalization of land and industry; solidarity with all oppressed groups.[1] Although there are significant differences between Vargas's populism in Brazil in the thirties, Peron's in Argentina in the forties, and other populist governments such as those in Chile, Colombia, and Uruguay, on the whole one can accept José Comblin's general characterization of these populist movements:

> They are all an attempt to join the oppressed classes with the new progressive and modern classes; to form a coalition of peasants, workers, intellectuals, and "national bourgeoisie" against the traditional oligarchy and its foreign allies. The method proposed is threefold: nationalization of foreign manufactures, mining, public services, and the land (agrarian reform); modernization of life and industrialization by the creation of national industry; and social reform and collective social conventions.[2]

THE THIRD COLONIAL PACT

The international economic and political conditions that paved the way for the emergence of populism did not last long enough to allow for its evolution into a new pattern for organizing society (this oft-made point is purely hypothetical anyway inasmuch as internal contradictions within the project might have rendered it nonviable in any case). At the end of World War II the international capitalist system, led by the U.S., was ready to regain and reshape its worldwide economic and political domination. The U.S. emerged from the war as the undisputed world power: it had sustained the fewest human losses, fought outside its own mainland territories, and kept its productive apparatus and economic-financial power intact while all the other countries (on both sides of the conflict) were being severely ravaged.

This emergence of the so-called Western world under the leadership of the U.S. lends credence to the thesis that in capitalist social formations the economic factor plays the predominant role. What takes place following World War II is, in effect, a major reaccommodation of capitalism, the chief feature of which is the integration of productive capital—and eventually also of financial and commercial capital—on an international scale. The transnational corporation (TNC) represents the culmination of that development. TNCs seek ever-increasing profits through an ever-expanding control of the international market. Oligopoly or monopoly control assures profits which satisfy the stockholders and guarantee success in the worldwide competition among TNCs. The degree of concentration achieved in this way is extraordinary and can easily be documented. The consequence is that the so-called capitalist *laws* of supply and demand become less and less significant; indeed, at the world level there is practically no free interplay of supply and demand because in this one integrated space that is the world economic order prices are not determined by supply and demand but by the power of the different agents—those states and coalitions of states and TNCs that operate in this "space."[3]

In such a situation it also becomes necessary to protect this "space" and to make it free for the operation of the TNCs. Thus, a whole system of military defense is organized and put in place in Europe, the Near East, the Far East, and Latin America. The doctrine developed to undergird and justify such a system has been articulated at the National War College (in Washington, D.C.), which was founded in 1948 for the preparation of the Joint Chiefs of Staff but has included in its seminars hundreds of outstanding leaders from a variety of professions. We shall have occasion already in our next section to return to the contents of this doctrine. For the present it is sufficient simply to recall such facets of it as geopolitical control, total war, and power as the basis of national security. The so-called cold war was the background against which this ideology was first developed. It is this coalition of economic and military power that prompted President Dwight Eisenhower's warning about the "military-industrial complex" threatening to take control.

How does this economic-military process impact the undeveloped and underdeveloped sections of the capitalist world (the countries usually called the Third World)? The old colonial system of direct political and economic domination is now anachronistic; even the neocolonial pact based on the exhange of raw materials and manufactured goods no longer suffices in the new situation. Instead there emerges what is usually referred to as the third colonial pact.

In a first stage, under the Kennedy administration, this third colonial pact creates the so-called development model (in Latin America "The Alliance for Progress") which tries to build on the "progressive" nationalist/populist movements with their project of industrialization, the welfare state, and alliance of the classes. The failure of this attempt has been recounted many times and need not be rehearsed here. The reasons for the failure have to do with the intrinsic incorrectness of the model, the conflict between the interests of the national bourgeoisie and those of the popular classes, the disappearance of the domestic markets, and, above all, the pressures of an international system that needs to occupy and integrate the entire space of the whole world economy.

This failure of the development model triggers a crisis. The national bourgeoisie reestablishes its traditional connection with international capital. Brazil can serve as an example. Around 1955 TNC investment begins to pour into Brazil. The national bourgeoisie is co-opted. Production is determined not by the needs of the Brazilian population but by those of the international market. The country soon becomes an outpost of the integrated world economy—and the Brazilian people a part of the global reservoir of cheap labor. It is at this point that some sectors of the populist forces become radicalized: they see where the process is leading, deepen their analysis of dependence as it relates to domestic conflict among the classes within the underdeveloped countries, and adopt an explicitly socialist project together with the new political strategies and tactics needed to carry it out. In some cases the populist governments themselves move radically to the left—for example, Goulart in Brazil, Torres in Bolivia, and the early Peronist government of Campora in Argentina. In Chile in 1971 a left-wing coalition brings Salvador Allende to power. Revolutionary groups emerge in such countries as Uruguay and Colombia, and also in Central America.

Thus the stage is set for the national security state. José Comblin, who has made a most careful study of this question, summarizes the relationship between the third colonial pact and the national security state:

> In the mid-1960s a new agreement arose between the traditional Latin American oligarchies and a new colonial power—the multinational corporations, especially the American-based ones. The United States ceased promoting democracy; the oligarchy recaptured the power in its own nations with the help of the multinational corporations. The agreement between oligarchy and international corporations promoted and continues to maintain military dictatorships all over Latin America. The myth of total war against communism hides the awareness of an opposition between developed and underdeveloped countries. The ideology of the colonial pact uses the vocabulary of development, while avoiding any contagion of nationalism or independence.[4]

NATIONAL SECURITY

What is the doctrine of "national security" and how does it operate? In spite of its negligible value intellectually, for philosophical purposes, the doctrine of national security provides a strong and coherent justification for the new military regimes. Historically it can be traced back to romantic-idealist ideologues of Pan-Germanism in the nineteenth century (studied, for instance, in the U.S. by Brian Mahan). Taken up in the Nazi period, it underwent a pragmatic elaboration by the American military establishment in the security ideology of the cold war.[5] It has also been variously embraced by such Latin American military ideologues as Gen. Golbery da Silva in Brazil, Augusto Pinochet in Chile, and Osiris Villegas in Argentina.

Basic to the doctrine is the notion that the state is an organism with a life of its own. This conception of the state, in turn, evokes two further ideas. The first has to do with the integrity of such an organism: the state consists of a territory, a population, and sovereignty—the last of the three elements being naturally the decisive one. The preservation and enhancement of sovereignty determines the use of the territory and the organization of the population. Besides the idea of integrity there is the idea of the growth of such an organism: every state is in permanent conflict with others in order to extend its Lebensraum and to impose on them its will.

This organic view of the state has a number of corollaries: (1) The key concept is power—"the ability of the state to make its own will reality."[6] (2) The main operative concept is strategy—the organization of domestic affairs and foreign relations in such a way that power may operate most efficiently in the achievement of the "interests" of the state. (3) The permanent condition is total war, that is, a war that is carried on at all levels—military, ideological, political, economic—and engages all the forces and resources of the state. (4) A strong, coherent, and committed elite is needed in order to wage this war, which requires a total concentration of power. (5) The goal of this struggle is the state itself—the visible and operative form of the nation—and hence "national interest" or "the essence of nationhood" or "the national being" becomes in effect identical with the strength and growth of the state. Certain observations can be made concerning the operation of this ideology in Latin America and in Third World countries generally. Three are particularly important.

First, this doctrine of national security is rarely made explicit in countries dominated by the military. In many such countries, in fact, the doctrine is *explicitly* rejected. Nevertheless, a careful study of the public declarations, laws and decrees, and institutions of such military governments immediately shows their *implicit* acceptance and use of national security doctrine. No one therefore should be deceived by their language about freedom and democracy, which at the operational level is reinterpreted in terms of the ideology of national security.

Second, although the terminology we have been using for purposes of theoretical definition is deliberately abstract, all these categories are precisely articulated in specific historical situations: it is the Christian West that is engaged in mortal struggle against materialistic and atheistic communism. This war must engage all the resources of the Western countries. Only the military is able to safeguard the security of the Western world. Hence the military must exercise—whether directly in government or indirectly through institutional participation in power—a vigilance function. A "strong" state must exercise total control; where the waging of this war is at stake, the state must suppress all dissent.

Third, it becomes clear that this national security ideology plays a diversionary role, as a cover for and in the service of the economic hegemony of multinational capitalism (which is in no way to deny the sincerity of some of its believers). In fact, the nationalistic rhetoric of the military governments is in practice clearly undermined by the total sellout of their own national economies to the transnational interests. The new military rulers are no longer the individualistic colonels or generals of the traditional *cuartelazos*[7] but a technocratic-bureaucratic elite. Educated in the American military academies, they act as guardians of the TNCs and implementers of the economic philosophy of the Chicago school of economics.

The International Commission of Jurists in 1976 prepared a study on military regimes in Latin America in which they summarized the main features of the juridical structure adopted by these regimes. They present their report under nine headings, the mere enumeration of which is enough to suggest how these regimes operate: (1) juridical mechanisms of repression—to create "emergency" legislation that suspends constitutional guarantees; (2) new governmental institutions—basically "boards of national security" with authority extending to all areas of national life; (3) suspension of the electoral process and designation of the chief executive by military juntas or similar bodies; (4) dismissal of legislative bodies (parliaments) and proscription of all political activity—sometimes also the creation of military "legislative bodies"; (5) limitations on the organization of labor and restrictions of the right of association; (6) control of the press and other means of communication; (7) restrictions on cultural freedom, such as the prohibition of books and ideological censorship of art; (8) military courts that extend their jurisdiction to include civilians and that suppress habeas corpus and other legal protections. The Commission's final summary deserves to be quoted in full:

> As has been shown, the general tendency of all these countries is identical or very similar; they all intend to establish and consolidate authoritarian and anti-juridical regimes, controlled and directed by the armed forces. This evolution is not capricious. It has been applied with the purpose of establishing a new power structure which brings with it the destruction of the traditional democratic system and the elimination of all forms of opposition.[8]

We can easily discern behind all this abstract and careful language the tragic story of countless real-life atrocities, a story which has shocked the world.

"SECURITY" AND RELIGION

The relevance of these insights for our general subject becomes evident when we realize how much stress these military regimes place on the religious dimension. The question is itself deserving of a full-length study. Since this is not possible here, I will limit myself to a few observations.

The rhetoric used by the military regimes abounds in religious references. It defines their aim as the defense of Christian civilization and the struggle against atheism and materialism. It extols religious values, particularly those of family and the religious tradition. It uses highly religious language in characterizing its goals in the war against subversion—sacred, cult, sacrifice, redeeming, martyrs, purging—and in the denunciation of its enemies and their acts—diabolic, sacrilegious, anti-Christian, satanic.

More important, the regimes include religious teaching in one form or another as a part of their educational program. Perhaps a simple quotation from the Brazilian education act (a law dictated by the Brazilian government early in its program) will illustrate the careful blending of political and religious ideology. The law says that the object of the educational process is "to idealize [sic] religion, morality, and civic virtue as defining three concentric circles, of which religion is the outer, morality the intermediate, and civic virtue the inner one. In this way, civic duties, rights, and acts are a part of larger moral duties, rights, and acts; and morality is bound to permanent principles originating in God." Elsewhere in the same document the interconnection is made explicit in several ways: the chain moves from the abstract/external/universal to the concrete/immediate/enforceable; from the God-religion-morality scale of values to social institutions—the present development plans (of the Brazilian government)—the integration (of Brazil) into the Western world.[9]

Why are these authoritarian regimes so concerned about a religious foundation? The answer to this question has to do with what Fals-Borda calls "the mechanisms of compulsion" that are needed in order to "institutionalize"—to make permanent—a new organization of society.[10] He mentions three main ones: (1) hegemonic domination—a government team whose members "think similarly regarding social and economic transformation" and have the power to implement it; (2) leadership ability—a well-trained, competent, and politically sophisticated group of leaders; and (3) social diffusion—a process for carrying "its ideology to all levels of the society." Fals-Borda adds as factors of stabilization, among others, "the legitimation of coercion." We can hardly deny that the military regimes indeed manifest the first two of Fals-Borda's "mechanisms." But "legitimation" and "social diffusion" remain—for them—crucial unsolved problems. Large sectors of the population—particularly the lower strata—remain impervious to their propaganda and silently hostile to their domination. In a continent where religion plays such an important role, and where it has so consistently operated to buttress the established order, the churches would seem to be a natural ally of the authoritarian governments. After all, church and government supposedly both have in atheistic Marxism a common enemy; they also have a common concern for an ordered and stable society. For these reasons the cooperation of the church was long taken for granted by these governments. The religious-ethical-social doctrines to which we have been referring were supposed to express the church-government relationship and to ensure the common religious-political project.

But it has not happened that way. On the contrary, after a brief period, the Roman Catholic Church and some Protestant churches began increasingly to criticize the authoritarian regimes and their official doctrine. This is not the place to enter into a detailed history of this developing estrangement, which will no doubt constitute one of the most significant events in twentieth-century church history, but at least it can be said that the process is by no means a uniform one. Few churches have reached the clarity and depth of some critical documents of the Brazilian Episcopal Conference. Some Catholic and Protestant laity and bishops are explicitly aligned with the governments. But the "protest within" (*contestation*) and the radical protest (*protestation*)—to use again the Desroche terminology—are strong enough to constitute the most visible profile of Christianity in Latin America today. It is, therefore, necessary to sketch some of the reasons which—at the human level—explain this atypical behavior of the churches. The reasons fall into three categories:

First, there are the institutional considerations. As the state assumes the role of interpreter and teacher of religion (usually under the rubric of civil ethics or civil morality or civil and moral education) it becomes a kind of parallel magisterium that endangers the unity and cohesion of the church. This is particularly true as regards the Roman Catholic Church.

Second, there are the doctrinal considerations. The understandings of the nature of human life, of society, of the state, and of freedom that prevail in the national security state prove incompatible with Christian doctrine as understood in both Protestant and Catholic thinking. In this respect, the social teaching of the Church developed in Catholicism during the last hundred years (which in other respects we have criticized) has proved to be, at least in the initial phases of the conflict, a powerful weapon against the pagan doctrine of the national security state. A paganism which idolizes power and reduces the person to an instrument of the expansion of the state can hardly be reconciled with the humanistic thrust of the classical "natural law."

Finally, there are the pastoral considerations—and these are of two sorts: On the one hand, Christian concern for the life and welfare of the people drives the church to denounce the violation of human rights and the policies that exacerbate the condition of the poor. On the other hand—and this could be called a strategic consideration—the church, particularly the Roman Catholic Church, discerns quite clearly the impossibility of relating positively *at one and the same time* both to the authoritarian state and to the people, particularly to those popular majorities whom the state represses, impoverishes, and marginalizes. The church cannot but perceive that to the degree it is seen by the people as an ally of the authoritarian governments its pastoral access to the masses is reduced.

THE SHARPENING OF THE DILEMMA

Our historical sketch has brought us to the threshold where the present comes smack up against the future. But even on this side of that frontier, one thing is already plain to see—the failure of the national security state. Perhaps the most visible sign of this failure is the bankruptcy of the economic plans adopted by these governments, plans that were shaped in keeping with the theories of the Chicago school of economics and imposed by the international financial institutions. So total is the bankruptcy that these economic plans have not only proved unable to incorporate actively the majority of the population and to provide even minimal levels of social progress; they have also thrown the countries into economic paralysis, destroying their productive capacity and creating colossal external debts that threaten the entire international financial system. Both in relative terms and in absolute terms all the indicators are negative. The appeal to the *future* and the rhetoric about the need for sacrifice in the short run have lost all their force. After an almost fifteen-year "economic miracle" Brazil woke up once again to social conflicts, uncontrollable inflation, and massive poverty. Argentina, Uruguay, and Chile, which have followed the model even more closely, find themselves in even worse shape—and in a shorter time!

Political failure adds to the crisis. A military establishment that wields political power cannot but internalize the conflicts of a society in which it closes all avenues for public expression and participation. For all the establishments' claims of monolithic unity and their attempts to hide internal disagreements, the economic failure and the tensions within the society are reflected and refracted within the armed forces as well (the process has been studied in Greece, Spain, and Portugal). The prospect of having to exercise permanent repression in order to deal with permanent unrest is demoralizing. This in turn alienates the transnational economic interests and their national allies, who cannot function properly in a climate of tension, unrest, and conflict. The "trilateral" program of "democratization" which the Carter administration intended to push through in Latin America may now be weakened or modified, but it represents a genuine need of the world capitalist system and it will continue to exercise pressure on the military governments.

Most importantly, there are the people. A Brazilian paper some months ago carried a cartoon in which the president is calling on the economics minister. The president says: "The inflation is creating unrest among the people; we have to eliminate it." "Sir," answers the economics minister, "would it not be easier to eliminate the people?" Here is the crux of the problem: an underprivileged minority can be accommodated in a relatively affluent economy. Or it can be repressed violently—even the genocide of a tribe or ethnic group has been envisaged as "justifiable." But it is not possible permanently to repress or eliminate the large and growing majority of the people. As the economy abroad, in worldwide crisis, continues to export inflation, insecurity, and unemployment to the Third World, and as the domestic conditions of appropriation and distribution compound the crisis, social unrest and conflict are bound to escalate. A regime that has nothing but sheer repressive force on which to rely is ultimately doomed—even if in the short run it manages to create untold misery, suffering, and death.

The more enlightened members of the military governments are by no means unaware of this prognosis. That awareness accounts for their attempts to find political solutions which, while institutionalizing and thus ensuring the continuity of their project, will develop a societal base strong enough to minimize the need for active coercion: They make changes in the constitution. They assign a permanent role to the military in any institutionalized government as a kind of backup insurance. They attempt to create center-right political coalitions that will look favorably on the military ideas. All these approaches have been tried in the effort to create qualified democracies—variously named strong, limited, stable—that can serve as successors to the "exceptional regimes." It is precisely this effort to elaborate such plans, to specify forms and schedules of transition to the next stage, that fosters some of the internal tensions now plaguing the military regimes. So far none of the regimes has been able to come up with an acceptable model for, much less effect a successful transition to, a successor government.[11]

I can hardly claim for this fragmentary historical survey any value except as a hypothesis that may help us in our inquiry. Moreover, while I have tried to restrict the survey to Latin American history, developments there are surely not an isolated experience. Basic elements of that history as uncovered by our survey are doubtless to be found in other situations as well, albeit in different configurations.

To the extent that the hypothesis is true, we can characterize the present situation (with all the caveats that necessarily attend such a formulation) as a time of transition—not just in some vague general sense but as a historical watershed between two social formations. The liberal modernization project, as incorporated in the liberal democratic state built on the base of free-enterprise capitalism, seems to have run its course and proven unable to respond to the needs of humanity at the present stage of human development. The situation today is unstable socially, economically, and politically. If history moves in quest of the new, what are the projects that today invite our response? What are the *priorities* that we can *identify,* amongst which we will have to choose ethically?

The capitalist transnational project with its technocratic ideology presents itself as the "natural" extension of and successor to the liberal democratic society. In the Third World, this project is represented by the technocratic-oligarchic elites that have by military means taken control of the mechanisms of the state. The two characteristic features of their project seem to be controlled development within the frame-work of the world capitalist system, and limited democracy under the management of technocratic elites. In the countries that dominate this world capitalist system, even though the conditions and mechanisms differ, it is possible to discern corresponding lines of a similar model.

Ethical considerations apart—as far as our present objective of historical identification is concerned—there seem to be two main obstacles to the realization of this project, one economic, the other political. Economically the capitalist transnational system has found it increasingly difficult to incorporate "peripheral economies" into the whole system in a socially and economically acceptable manner. In fact, the "central" economies themselves find it increasingly difficult to provide conditions for the full participation of all sectors of their own society in the productive process. Politically it has proved impossible to co-opt the popular majorities of the Third World into the modernizing project. The sheer pressure of these vast and increasing populations—not to speak of such sectors of the central countries themselves as the young and the unemployed—tends to destabilize the political situation. Either it generates the kind of unrest and violence that threaten democratic life, or it justifies the centralization of power, tightened state control, and enhanced repression, whether hidden or overt—which also amounts to the demise of the democratic liberal project.

The attempt to enforce this capitalist transnational project, in fact to transform the whole world into one massive security state—should it be called an empire?—has already by a process of action and reaction unleashed armed conflicts in many areas of the world. Indeed it now threatens to kindle a global conflict in which the risk of annihilation faces all of civilization, if not human life itself.

On the other hand, it is not difficult to perceive the manifestations of what we have earlier called, in relation to Latin America, a project of liberation. This project is not a unified and homogeneous program. Still undefined in its technical aspects, clearly taking different form in the different regional and national situations, and certainly varied in emphasis, it should perhaps be spoken of in the plural as projects of liberation. Clearly identifiable in this plurality, however, are common basic features and, above all, an almost instinctive sense of common commitment. What is involved here is not a utopia—though the project has utopian dimensions—but a diverse movement with so many fundamental common options as to justify our use of the singular in referring to it.

Gustavo Gutiérrez has tried to summarize these common options in a fourfold formula: (1) societal appropriation of the means of production; (2) societal appropriation of political power (his expression is "political management," *gestión*); (3) societal appropriation of freedom; and (4) the creation of a new social consciousness.[12] This characterization, which I fully endorse, deserves at least three comments.

First, we can easily see the "utopian" concern that inspires this liberation project—the desire to undo the personal and social alienation humans have experienced in relation to the world (the means of production), society (political power), and culture (freedom). The new consciousness has reference to a communal awareness in which human beings, in the totality of their individual life and their social life, repossess their own being. This utopian vision can be viewed and interpreted with reference to the history of humanistic Western culture, but it can also be read theologically in the light of such symbols as the kingdom of God and the New Creation.

Second, the fourfold formula points to concrete historical features in the emerging new society. It points to a society which can be described as socialist in the organization of its economy, democratic in terms of the political participation of the people, and open in the sense of ensuring the conditions for personal realization, cultural freedom and opportunity, and the mechanisms for self-correction.

Third, although such features are concrete enough to suggest a certain type of society to the exclusion of others, they still leave room for a number of specific options, such as various forms of societal appropriation of the means of production, gradations of interplay between central planning and group and individual initiative, diverse models of political participation, and the possibility of intermediate organizations in the various areas of culture. Such imprecision is not accidental. It expresses the recognition that, within this basic historical project of liberation, there is the possibility of—indeed the need for—consideration of varying circumstances and diverse national or regional conditions and possibilities of implementation. The people's movements in Asia, the liberation struggles in Africa, and the different political alternatives being pursued in Latin America today represent a wide variety of choices, but all can be recognized as—and in many cases they recognize themselves to be—"a family of options" representative of a specific historical project.

To decide in favor of such a project of liberation raises the question of "transition," a question that involves at least two difficult aspects. On the one hand, the method for transition will not be easy to establish since the capitalist transnational project, as experience clearly shows, will not spare any effort—however costly in human terms—to block all attempts at effecting qualitative change. Consideration must be given to the space available for effective transformation, the need for intermediate stages and political alliances, and the possibilities for popular mobilization—all those factors that enter into the determination of concrete alternatives for immediate political action. Here, naturally, there will be diversity of proposals and, not infrequently, sharp disagreements and internal conflicts among the forces of change. On the other hand, since we are dealing with the creation of a *new* model, there is a wide margin for the unpredictable. When the future is seen as a mere extrapolation from the present, futurology can function as a technical tool, since it works only with known data (fortunately, reality has often given the lie to such scenarios). But when the future is an authentic hope struggling to become historical, when we opt for a truly qualitative change, the validity of the option can be established only in its realization, that is, by means of political praxis.

We have come now *as far as the historical identification of priorities can carry us.* The hypothesis that our analysis is true puts sharply before us a concrete historical alternative with its manifold possibilities, uncertainties, and dead ends. We have to make choices in terms of both the global historical project and the specific courses of action. If there is a direction in which this identification of possibilities and choices points us, it is not unambiguous or "scientifically" beyond question. We are now in the realm of commitment and praxis. Here we must pay attention to what Paul Lehmann called the "theological determination" of priorities.

6

Justice and Order

Immanuel Kant asked a fundamental question: "What ought I to do?" We could paraphrase that in terms of a Christian ethics: "What ought I, a Christian, to do?"—specifically (in terms of our present context) in relation to political life. To have addressed this question at the outset would have been to short-circuit the ethical issue by trying to circumvent the determinations of reality. In other words, it would have given us an idealistic ethics. Now, however, after having tried to explore "the historical identification of priorities," we are in a position where we must face up to "the theological determination": "What should I, *a Christian*, do?" This is the point at which we move beyond a mere preface to theological ethics and get to the very substance of it.

To make this move properly, we would have to develop both an overall systematic approach and a theological analysis of the whole set of ethical problems that are connected with politics. Obviously, we will not be able to do that in the present context. Such an effort requires a long and cooperative endeavor on the part of many Christian theologians for some time to come. So, if I may be permitted to prolong the metaphor, I will try merely to suggest a "table of contents"—at least the main chapters—for such a development, as I see it now from the perspective that I have tried to sketch in the preceding pages.

There are those, no doubt, who would say that, as Christians, we do not have any special criteria for arriving at political decisions. Some would even say, perhaps more frequently, that we cannot establish any generally valid criteria for Christians in the political sphere—there is simply a multiplicity of unreconciled options, among which Christians make good-faith choices, and that's the end of the matter. But what do they mean by that? If what they mean is that, subjectively, Christians can in good faith make—and have made—contradictory choices and that we cannot anticipate God's judgment about those choices, I would certainly agree. If they mean that, normally, political positions should

79

not be dogmatically prescribed by the church but rather developed in open discussion, study, and even confrontation, I would again agree. If they mean there is no such thing as a specifically Christian political platform, I agree. But if they mean that there are no Christian criteria whatever, that right and left can both be equally justified, that we are stranded in the quicksands of political relativism, and that the Scriptures are—as Luther in irony once put it—"a wax nose" that can be twisted in any direction, then I would most vigorously disagree. If we can give "a reasonable account of our hope" (1 Pet. 3:15), then we can also give account of our "walking" and our "conversation"—that is, our "praxis" in the world.

THE MOST MATERIALIST OF
ALL RELIGIONS

Biblical and theological scholarship over the past fifty years has clearly established that dichotomies between the inner life and the outward life, the spiritual and the material, the individual and the communal, theology and ethics—dichotomies on which much of theology and particularly much of modern theology has been built—are foreign to the basic outlook of biblical thought. We can safely begin, therefore, with the assertion that any theological ethics deserving of the name biblical has to honor what we call the incarnational perspective. This is what Archbishop Temple meant when he said fifty years ago (perhaps quoting Dostoyevsky) that Christianity could claim to be "the most avowedly materialist" of all religions[1]; or what Karl Barth meant when toward the end of his theological pilgrimage he said that "the humanity of God" is the basic criterion for understanding God's revelation. Naturally the reference here is not merely to the Incarnation as an isolated event, a sort of abrupt departure from God's "normal" way of dealing with human life and reality. On the contrary, the Incarnation becomes the clue for understanding all of God's dealings with human history and with the whole of world reality. It speaks, on the one hand, of God's "free affirmation of man, his free concern for him, his free substitution for him," as Barth expresses it.[2] On the other hand, it commits Christians, as Temple himself puts it, to "belief in the ultimate significance of the historical process."[3]

Bonhoeffer has forcefully expressed the unavoidable tension implicit in such an incarnational perspective when, in his quest for the foundations of a Christian ethics, he says: "The form of Christ certainly is and remains one and the same, yet it is willing to take form in the real man, that is to say, in quite different guises. Christ does not dispense with human reality for the sake of an idea which demands realization at the expense of reality. What Christ does is precisely to give effect to reality. He affirms reality. And indeed he is himself the real man and consequently the foundation for all human reality."[4] Only a fully trinitarian theology can give meaning to such an incarnational approach, because only such a theology can fully respect both the autonomy of reality and history (what in traditional language we could call "the distinction of the persons" of the Trinity) and the dynamic normativeness of the once-for-all Incarnation of the Word in Jesus of Nazareth ("the unity of substance" to retain the classical expression).[5] An incarnational ethics would therefore affirm: (1) the ultimacy of the christological determination of ethical priorities, whereby Jesus Christ in his historical and permanent ministry is the measure and the power of God's purpose in the world; and (2) the significance of historical action and fulfillment as assumed in God's permanent concern, initiative, and action for humanization in history.

The tension appears when, granting the validity of these theological affirmations, we try to make explicit their concrete significance for political life. How can we relate the specific reference to a particular history (that of Jesus Christ) to our own contemporary history? What is the hermeneutical mediation for a "theological determination of priorities"? Paul Lehmann himself takes the following direction:

> A theology of Incarnation affirms that the presence of Jesus of Nazareth in the human story *opens up a way of perceiving* the world of time and space and things *that gives primacy and priority to* the human sense and significance of what is going on.[6]

If we ask how does this happen, the answer is:

> This apperception, sensibility, and way of thinking do not interpret the goings-on in the world of time and space and things "off the pages of the Bible," as it were. Nor do they interpret the Bible "off the pages" of the daily goings-on in the world of time and space and things.[7]

Lehmann then appeals to "an insight of faith nurtured in the Christian community in the world"[8] and uses the illustration of the "tropical" (from *tropos* = metaphorical) interpretation of the Bible by the Fathers.[9] I would not wish to question the importance of this "discernment." In fact, it seems to me a much-needed insight, one that the so-called objective historical-critical interpretation has discarded to the detriment of both our theology and our hermeneutics. And I fully agree with the "humanist" direction and the ethical criteria that Lehmann indicates. But it seems to me that a greater claim can be made for the guidance to be had "off the pages of the Bible."

HERMENEUTICS BETWEEN ORDER
AND JUSTICE

Augustine of Hippo was one of the first theologians to make a systematic effort to discern at a particular point in human history "the presence of Jesus of Nazareth in the human story." Augustine asks the right question: how is God's sovereignty—his kingdom, his city— present and active in the events of history? Augustine saw history as the place where God's city and the human city intersect, struggle, and move toward their particular appointed goals. Justice and love are the two foundations of the eternal city that impinge on the earthly one. On the one hand, it is justice that gives legitimacy to any human sovereignty, that establishes the right of the earthly city. If justice is taken away, says Augustine—literally, "in the absence of justice"—"what is sovereignty" (or kingdoms) but great robberies, "organized brigandage?"[10] On the other hand, love is the inner motivation, the basic impulse for human life; properly oriented, it invariably points the direction for human action. That is why one can act freely out of love: "Love and do what you want." Justice (the objective basis) and love (the motivating force) together offer a hermeneutical key that enables us to discern God's active presence in history and to determine our Christian praxis accordingly.

So far so good. But then Augustine meets some concrete practical problems and his responses reveal the presence of yet another herme- neutical key which, as I see it, empties the first key of much of its meaning. In discussing the punishment inflicted on the Donatists, for example, Augustine deals on several occasions with the question of property rights. For him, naturally, everything finally belongs to God—God is ultimately the only legitimate owner. But men are entitled to call some goods their own when they possess them "rightly" (*juste*); on the other hand, anything possessed "badly" cannot be called one's own, and "that is possessed badly which is badly used." On that basis, many who possess much could be "rightly" dispossessed, says Au- gustine.[11] However, side by side with this "divine right" by virtue of which man rightly possesses what he has rightly acquired and properly uses, there is as a matter of fact also "a human right which is at the mercy of the rulers of the earth."[12] To be sure, these two rights do not coincide. God's justice stands critically over against the status quo. There is a tension between the eschatological kingdom and the earthly "arrangements." "Meanwhile, the wickedness of bad possessors is tolerated, not because in that way one might make them into good possessors but in order that, even though they use these possessions badly, they may be less of a nuisance."[13]

In Augustine's view, true balance, proper restitution, will take place only when we arrive at "that city wherein lies our eternal heritage." Apart from the specific occasion of these reflections (in which Augustine is in fact advocating leniency toward the heretics) his statements express what has become almost a constant in Christian social thinking: many things are badly ordered in "the earthly city"; those who are entitled to enjoy certain things do not have them, and vice versa; some people are unjustly treated; innocents are sometimes tortured as criminals—all of these instances are cited by Augustine himself. Such injustices should be corrected whenever that can be done *without endangering order and peace*. But if any redress of wrong threatens to become disruptive, it should be avoided.

The premise of Augustine's position in these cases is quite clear— peace understood as order. Society is an organism that must function harmoniously. The chief purpose of societal organization is the suppression of conflict and tumult. Changes, or the respect for personal freedom or for justice, might endanger that order. Whenever an alternative emerges, therefore, the Christian ought to work for the best possible solution, the most just and generous one, *short of endangering the existing order*.

There is, no doubt, a certain anthropological and historical pessimism underlying such a view. More important, however, is to see in it a concept of order and of peace that goes back to the classical Greco-Roman tradition, which compares society to a living organism (in Plato or Aristotle "the celestial order"), in which the basic "organs" or "parts" are *naturally* determined and regulated—government and subjects, slaves and citizens, men and women. Any basic change in these functions and relations is, therefore, a crime against nature (translated into the terms of Christian theology, "a rebellion against creation"). Peace, therefore, understood as order is the basic direction, the ultimate ethical key. Theologically, justice and love are supreme, but historically both are subordinated to order.

Behind this theological-ethical perspective, we must see a sociopolitical fact: the church has accepted the role of supporting, sustaining, and guiding the state. To that degree, Christianity has in fact become a "political religion" and its theology a "political theology." True, such theology differs from the political theology of the classic Greco-Roman tradition because it cannot completely silence the tension created by its eschatological reference—the "heavenly city" wherein justice dwells.

But, within this eschatological limitation, the church's theology fulfills a function similar to that of the ancients: it establishes the existing order. To be sure, it tries to humanize it, to curb its abuses, to Christianize it. But ultimately the church takes responsibility for the existing order, and hence it will not undertake to foster or accept radical change. Indeed, change is seen as the onslaught of chaos and must be resisted at all costs.

It is easy to see that most of the models for political ethics that we identified above in chapter 2 have operated within this premise concerning the relation between justice and order. Paul Lehmann refers to "the line" that is drawn "between a self-justifying perpetuation of power at the service of the established order and a revolutionary use of power for the liberation of man for human fulfillment."[14] Christian ethics—however idealistic—has operated "at the service of the established order." When the "direction," the basic thrust of the theological determination of priorities is "order" so conceived, both love and justice lose their critical power.

THE ORDER OF JUSTICE

Although we must admit that this tradition of "order" has been dominant in the history of the church since at least the fifth century, it is also necessary to emphasize that there has at the same time always been another tradition as well, sometimes very small and even marginal to the ecclesiastical structure, one that has interpreted the Bible in another direction—as a call to radical transformation inspired by the prophetic-messianic focus on the justice and peace of the kingdom of God. Whatever excesses or distortions we may find in it, the alternative tradition witnesses to a biblical line that present-day scholarship has vindicated as central. The works of Gerhard von Rad in Old Testament, of Ernst Käsemann in New Testament, and of European "political theology" and the "theology of hope" in dogmatics, to mention only a few of the best known, have shown the centrality and relevance of this tradition.

In this tradition, the eschatological kingdom is experienced and understood as constantly pressing to manifest itself in history, inviting people to enter obediently into the sphere of God's sovereignty on earth. Righteousness-justice is seen as the distinguishing characteristic of the kingdom—and hence as the mark of God's faithful action and people's correspondingly faith-ful obedience. The condition of the poor and oppressed in fact becomes the test of God's redeeming presence and of human justice.

God, accordingly, is seen as the redeemer, the liberator and avenger (*go'el*) of the oppressed. Such a view is not confined to the classical prophetic tradition. In different forms, and sometimes in the context of different theological outlooks, it appears as a motif in the laws protecting the unprotected (the orphan, widow, foreigner, dispossessed). The theological background of these laws is the idea of the covenant. God has promised to be the protector of the people—he becomes the "next of kin" of all Israelites—and the law ensures the means through which such protection is guaranteed. In the priestly tradition of Genesis 9, this covenant has a universal scope: God is the guarantor of all life, the avenger of all human blood, and he entrusts to man the exercise of this protective function.[15]

It is against this background of the covenant that we can understand the prophetic concept of justice. In the words of von Rad, "There is absolutely no concept in the Old Testament with so central a significance for all the relationships of human life as that of *tsedaqah*."[16] He hastens to add that this "righteousness" cannot be understood simply as a general norm or universal law; it is a relational concept. It has to do with the faithful fulfillment of those commitments that gain binding force within the established relationships—God and his people, the covenanted people themselves, and the whole of humankind in the universalistic interpretation of the covenant. God acts in righteousness when he establishes and reestablishes right relationships, restoring those who have been wronged in their legitimate claims as members of the covenant. Such action is the equivalent of "salvation." When God liberates Israel, when he protects the unprotected, when he delivers the captive or vindicates the right of the poor, he is exhibiting his justice.[17]

It has frequently been noted that kingship was always a somewhat alien entity in Israel, always in potential—and in many cases actual—conflict with God's sovereign right. Few kings escaped the critical evaluation of the prophets. Two interrelated criteria seem to govern such evaluations: (1) faithfulness to the exclusive claim of Jahweh and (2) the faithful exercise of justice, the test of which is concern for the poor and unprotected. In the context of the theology of the covenant, to which we have referred, these two criteria are inseparable; and in the prophetic pronouncements about specific kings the keeping of both and the breach of both go hand in hand. Only when the king fulfills the requirement of human justice is he a true representative of God's righteousness; at the point of such fulfillment the king manifests "the knowledge of the Lord." Nowhere is this more succinctly and forcefully expressed than in the oft-quoted words of Jeremiah spoken in judging Jehoiakim's rulership over against that of his father Josiah: "Did not your father [Josiah] eat and drink and do justice and righteousness [the

concrete acts and the corresponding relationships]? Then it was well
with him. He judged the cause of the poor and needy; then it was well"
(Jer. 22:15–16).

The "rights of the poor," as some early Fathers expressed it, become
therefore the criterion for right government. Clearly this is the way in
which Jesus himself interprets the impact of God's kingdom as he
announces and enacts it in his own ministry. And however we may
interpret it historically or theologically, this understanding of his message and mission was doubtless one of the decisive issues in the confrontation that brought him to his death.[18]

THE RIGHT ORDER OF PRIORITIES

If we accept this hermeneutical key for an understanding of the
theological determination of priorities, then the question of the Con-
stantinian church has to be turned completely around. The true question is not "What degree of justice (liberation of the poor) is compatible
with the maintenance of the existing order?" but *"What kind of order,
which order is compatible with the exercise of justice (the right of the
poor)?"* Here alone do we find an adequate point of departure for the
theological determination of priorities. The fixed point is "justice, the
right of the poor." This is the theological premise from which we cannot
depart. The variable to be explored has to do with the conditions and
possibilities of an order that can best bring that right to fulfillment. On
such a view, social change is taken for granted not as a good in itself (not
change just for the sake of change), but because it is implied in the search
for an order—which has to be a new order since the existing order does
not achieve this aim—in which this right of the poor takes precedence.

The concern for order has by no means disappeared. In fact, the
biblical concept of peace (*shalom*) includes well-ordered relationships,
stability—the "constants," or regularities (as Karl Barth calls them),
which make human life possible in a society. There is, for the Bible, an
order of creation and regularity, an organic character to human life in
the cosmos, which corresponds to God's faithfulness. The meaning and
direction of such order and regularity, however, is determined not by
some natural law (all too promptly equated with the status quo) but by
God's liberating righteousness operative in history and manifest in
Jesus Christ. "Peace," in the words of Isaiah, "is the fruit of righteousness"; order is at the service of freedom. This is the biblical order of
priorities. There are regularities, and they should be respected and
ensured. However, again with Barth, the first concern is for "the correctness of these regularities."[19] Justice is the foundation of order.

7

Hope and Power

The theological approach we have been sketching and the theological tradition that undergirds it have been frequently criticized or rejected as utopian—in more traditional language "enthusiastic" or "chiliastic." The attack has come recently from the advocates of "realism" in Christian political ethics and from theological purists who warn against confusing God's justice with human justice and against the kind of "activism" that might jettison the "eschatological reservation" and claim to build the kingdom of God through human effort. At this point I would therefore like to explore tentatively two issues which may help to clarify these questions—the issue of utopianism and the question of power.

THE REALISTIC EXORCIZING OF UTOPIA

Ethical realism, as pioneered in North American theology by Reinhold Niebuhr and John C. Bennett, has made a valuable contribution to the development of political ethics by its insistence on the use of analysis and on the search for historical mediation. Nevertheless, its mistrust of utopianism, developed in its critique of the Social Gospel, seems to have led it to capitulate before a form of pragmatism that plays into the hands of the status quo. Two brief examples may illustrate the point.

In an interesting article entitled "What Makes a Society Political?" Herbert W. Richardson makes a sharp distinction between two kinds of values—which he distinguishes as teleological and procedural.[1] Teleological values are those which "determine our . . . ultimate choices," our "conceptions of human happiness and fulfillment." Procedural (or structural) values determine "the way we organize society in order to decide and pursue our goals, and even "how we decide our teleological values." Political life, according to Richardson, has to do with the second, the procedural values—those organizational arrangements that a society establishes for itself. It should not contradict the teleological values, but is neither inspired nor corrected by them.

One may be surprised at Richardson's examples—for instance, "(valuing) private property" appears as a teleological value, while "differing views of man" seem to belong to the procedural values. But the basic thrust of his argument is clear: a society is merely an aggregate of individuals belonging to different types of primary institutions (family, neighborhood, church, trade), sometimes interpreted as "creational orders," that are held together as a society through some functional arrangements. On this view there is in society no intrinsic unity, no need to "agree with respect to teleological values": "A political society requires only that its members . . . be willing to interact politically enough to compromise their differences so that a social order can exist." In other words, a people does not exist as people: "Symbolizations of the origin and destiny of a people are not the common term that holds a political society together"; such teleological symbolizations "always presuppose that society is not a plurality of different agents, but a single organic whole." Richardson holds that such a society does need a "faith in the transcendent" (which is not necessarily a religious faith), but such faith acts only as a "critical principle" by relativizing all collective symbolizations; it guarantees "a private sphere."

I have paused here to summarize Richardson's view, not only because of its lucidity and directness but because it seems to offer a modern restatement of an older approach. Political life, on this view, is a series of convenient arrangements, presumably dictated by expediency, that are entered into in order to ensure the conditions for a life which will find its meaning and fulfillment elsewhere—in the private sphere and in those institutions where teleological values can be expressed. Theologically, therefore, the *polis*—society as such—is withdrawn not only from the creational order (the secularization here is more radical than in Luther) but also from the order of redemption, since the latter is supposedly concerned with teleological values. The "institutions"— presumably creational, to which the society as a whole would be "subsidiary"—are ruled in turn by a kind of law of nature. When we enquire where this "nature" is to be found, we are told—in an earlier Richardson book—that the future of the organization of society is determined by "sociotechnics":

> By sociotechnics is meant that new knowledge whereby man exercises technical control not only over nature but also over all the specific institutions that make up society: i.e., economics, education, science, and politics. Hence, sociotechnics presages the end of "economic man" as well as of "scientific man" and "political man." It replaces these separated institu-

tional functions with the cybernetic integration of society within a single rational system.[2]

Is this the final outcome of ethical realism? Richardson admits that he does not particularly like this "sociotechnical intellectus" but, recognizing "its inevitability," he feels that we should try to moralize it as much as possible.[3] Is this, then, what has become of the "theological determination"—accepting and moralizing the existing order? Ever since realism gave short shrift to the Social Gospel movement in America, that seems to have become—except for black theology during the last fifteen years—the dominant tendency in American political ethics. The painful movement of Reinhold Niebuhr (curiously paralleled in Europe by the evolution of Emil Brunner's "ethics of the orders") from a prophetic denunciation of "the immoral society" to the "realism" of the cold war seems to mark the way of a theology that tries to exorcise all "utopian" and "enthusiastic" tendencies in Christian political ethics: it results in dehistoricizing the kingdom of God and tolerating and justifying the injustices of the status quo—all in order to minimize offense.[4]

An energetic debate conducted in the pages of *Christianity and Crisis* in 1973 focuses this contrast. It originated in an article on the Latin American theology of liberation by journalist Thomas G. Sanders.[5] Such theology, for Sanders, represents a utopian attempt to make the kingdom of God a norm for Christian political ethics. This "soft utopianism" is mistaken, he says, both in its concept of man (it does not take sin seriously) and in its moralism (it does not recognize the ambiguous or ambivalent character of human decisions and actions). By using such concepts the liberation theologians presumably can be misleading when it comes to Christian political decision making: "Although concepts like liberation and the kingdom of God are legitimate symbols pointing to aspects of Christian faith and experience, they easily lead to greater confusion than enlightenment when intromitted into the political sphere as policy norms."[6] What then "must" (sic) the church do? It must operate within "a realistic approach," trying to improve existing conditions and to moralize the use of power, but recognizing the ambiguity of the situations and avoiding the dream of "revolutionary changes." In any case, "the church does not help by pointing to a religious reality *beyond the possibilities* of Latin American countries and making it into a political program. Rather, it must discern the moral implications underlying *existent societal processes* and alternative uses of power."[7]

In a harsh answer Rubem Alves tries to identify the difference between such realism and liberation theology. Certainly it is not a matter of the latter's "utopian" ignorance of the ambiguity of historical achievement. Utopianism (in the positive sense) "is not the belief in the possibility of a perfect society but rather the belief in the nonnecessity of *this* imperfect order." Liberation theology, according to Alves, recognizes the persistence of sin but also affirms:

> There is no reason for us to accept the rule of the sinful structures that now control reality. . . . What is at stake in the conflict between realism and utopianism is the way we read our Bibles. One alternative is to take the positivistic ideology as the ultimate horizon that provides the perspective for our thought, action, and reading of the Bible. The other alternative is to understand the claims of ultimacy of social reality as against the biblical horizons. . . . Utopianism . . . believes that somehow, somewhere, God is doing his thing: he is overthrowing the existing order. Therefore, it is necessary to debunk man-made realities."[8]

Our insistence on social analysis and historical mediation should make plain that we are not suggesting any short-circuiting of reality in political ethics. Certainly, it would be disastrous to "intromit" the kingdom of God into politics by way of "policy norms." The real question, however, is whether the kingdom of God is irrelevant to policy and therefore "existing social processes" are closed in themselves, or whether the kingdom is a horizon which commits us to an effort at transforming the "existing conditions" in its direction.

IS THE KINGDOM OF GOD A UTOPIA?

Ever since Marx drew a distinction between utopian socialism and scientific socialism, the discussion about the sociopolitical significance of utopian thinking has never ceased. Soviet communism has read Marx in the sense of an absolute rejection; in line with its positivistic and mechanistic interpretation, it has rejected all utopian thinking in the name of the so-called objective facts of the historical process. *Mutatis mutandis,* Althusser has done the same in the name of "scientific dialectical materialism." But the subjective reality thus suppressed or ignored will not disappear. Thus, within Marxism itself, significant voices have reinterpreted Marx and tried to recover the true meaning and significance of utopian thinking. I refer naturally to the so-called Frankfurt School and, above all, to the work of Ernst Bloch, whose *Prinzip Hoffnung* has also evoked a significant theological response. Aspects of Bloch's thought are significant for our present discussion.

(1) Utopia, according to Bloch, has three social functions: First, it represents protest against the present situation insofar as, by describing

a different situation, it denounces the negative aspects of things as they are. Second, it explores as yet unrealized possibilities in that it relates imagination and reality by projecting either in time (chiliasm) or in space (utopia more properly) a different reality. Third, it demands the immediate realization of such new society, without delay and intermediate stages, thus rejecting the "tyranny of reality" which the dominant ideologies try to impose. Mannheim had seen these functions but ascribed them to the "interests" of the conflicting classes and groups within a society. Bloch is not satisfied with this epistemological relativism. Utopian thinking, for him, is a way of knowing that corresponds to reality—to a tendency inherent in nature as well as in the human being. Reality must be understood against the horizon of its possibilities, in what has been called "an ontology of the not-yet." Utopia is not an illusion, it is knowledge—an anticipation of the possible future of reality.

(2) Not all utopian thinking belongs in this category. Bloch distinguishes between a kind of "naive optimism" (my expression) on the one hand, for which "everything is possible," without any consideration of objective factors, and, on the other hand, an anticipation which begins with a knowledge (more or less fragmentary or adequate) of reality. Such conception demands two philosophical presuppositions: first, to conceive of nature as a process containing within itself the possibilities of its own transformation; and second, to conceive of the human being as the midwife of this transformation, the complement of nature. This concrete, realistic utopianism accordingly would involve an anticipatory knowledge that is ultimately verified in human praxis. Bloch traces in different human manifestations, but particularly in religion—above all in the Jewish-Christian tradition—the presence of this "anticipatory consciousness" which, for him, has now to be "inherited," transformed, and realized in a true "dialectical materialism."

(3) Bloch is aware of an ultimate limit to all realistic utopias, even that of the classless society and the "kingdom of freedom." That limit is death itself. He deals with this question of death in several ways—from the classic Marxian response concerning death as the dissolving of the individual consciousness into the consciousness of humanity, to the consideration of death as the positive force of re-creation. I cannot discuss here either the coherence or the value of these interpretations. I wish only to emphasize the fact that Bloch is fully aware of the force of the negative in history and in reality. His is therefore not a triumphalist utopianism but a resolute invitation to anticipatory, realistic struggle spurred by hope.

Against the background of these general comments on utopia we can consider the question concerning the utopian dimension of the Christian faith, particularly—for our present purposes—the social significance of a Christian utopia and its place in a Christian political ethics. As we know, Marx and Engels had already called attention to the utopian significance of Christianity, but they interpreted it as "false consciousness." In Latin American liberation theology, on the other hand, there is a tendency to vindicate this Christian utopia as a mobilizing force. In some cases Christian exhortation uses eschatological motifs like "the new heaven and new earth" and "the new man" as Christian utopias that challenge us "in the construction of a new, more just, and more fraternal society."[9] In other cases, Christian eschatology is presented as a utopia inviting us to move toward it. Leonardo Boff, in particular, sees the resurrection of Christ as a "realized utopia," an anticipation of the goal of human history.[10]

For my part I would prefer, with Gustavo Gutiérrez and others, to establish a more indirect relation between utopia and the Christian faith. There are two reasons for this. In the first place, utopia is an ambiguous category to use in speaking of God's promise. Although we must recognize the utopian nature of eschatological categories and symbols, in eschatology we are not speaking of "human anticipations" but of God's time of consummation which, while it assumes history, does not simply crown history's achievements but also judges and transforms it. In the second place, to baptize as Christian the concrete utopias which emerge in the human quest is not only to ignore the qualitative newness of God's consummation but also to sacralize—and more seriously, to clericalize—human projects. The question is a complex and difficult one; I would only suggest some methodological points for approaching what I would call the utopia-genetic potentiality of Christian hope.

(1) Utopias are human creations. Both in the sense of utopian thinking and as concrete utopias, they have an important social function. Insofar as utopias extrapolate from reality by "negating the negative" and projecting human experiences of fulfillment, they are a powerful factor for change. Although one must be aware of the negative side— their ideological manipulation, the stimulation of a purely subjective voluntarism, the fanaticism that pretends to dispense with historical mediations—we must assign them, particularly the concrete or realistic utopias, a positive social and political value. We can concur with Paul VI who in his *Octogesima Adveniens* assigns them a role as protest against "bureaucratic socialism, technocratic capitalism, and au-

thoritarian democracy" and as "stimulating creative imagination to perceive ignored possibilities in the present and as orienting towards a new future." Through the confidence they give "to the creative forces of the human heart and spirit," he adds, utopias can "support the social dynamism."[11] In this sense, any particular historical project, while on the one hand related to the analysis of historical conditions, is on the other hand dependent on these utopian visions to project the shape of the society toward which it moves. In Latin America in particular it is the utopia of "a new man and a new society" which precedes the articulation of a historical project.[12]

(2) While we are speaking of utopias as human creations, we cannot ignore the historical relation of utopian thinking to religion; particularly in the West we must recognize the close link between a utopian imagination, which has been a dominant feature of our culture, and the Judeo-Christian tradition. Aspects of the biblical faith actually stimulate the creation of utopias. There is, in the first place, the belief in a power which unblocks the future, beyond its perceived limits. Whether we speak of *creatio ex nihilo,* the resurrection of Jesus, or the regeneration of human beings in the power of the Spirit, in each instance God appears as the negation of determinations. In such actions as the liberation of the people from Egypt or the overcoming of sterility in Sarah and Hannah promise and hope are the negation of natural impossibilities and of subjective cynicism.

(3) But such "breakthroughs" are not empty acts of power. They have a content, and they indicate a direction. The eschatological symbols sketch a picture which words charged with concrete meaning from the biblical story—words such as righteousness, peace, and life—try to convey. This picture acts critically as a judgment on existing conditions and it directs the imagination to extrapolate from present experience and project to the envisaged future dimensions that are congruous with it. This is clearly visible in the humanistic utopias of the Western world—and even, by contrast, in the negative utopias, such projections of the "antihuman" as Huxley's *Brave New World* and Orwell's *1984.*

(4) Besides judging existing conditions and pointing a direction, utopias may incite to action. Here the question is much more ambiguous: Does the Christian faith stimulate creative—utopian—political *praxis?* It is true that in the biblical story God's unblocking acts always constitute a call that engages and commits human beings to action. It is also true that the appeal to eschatological hope and the use of its symbols is frequently related to ethical questions—specific forms of action or resistance. But we cannot deny that in the history of Chris-

tianity the eschatological symbols have been so cut off from this world, so individualized, and so exclusively related to God's power conceived as the negation of human participation that they have led to resignation and historical cynicism. On the other hand, sometimes (as we have seen in Latin America) certain historical projects have been uncritically appropriated by Christians who are led into dubious commitments. We are faced at this point, therefore, with a double task: critical assessment in light of the direction pointed by the biblical prophetic-messianic tradition, and recovery of the praxis-provoking character of Christian eschatology, the dimension of call.

THE REALITY AND MYTH OF POWER

We have been speaking here about the political significance of hope and utopia. Power may seem to be at the other extreme of political reality; yet the two are closely related. As enabling, power is the possibility of hope's realization; as restricting, power is the limit of this possibility. We cannot, therefore, dodge the question of power in any treatment of political ethics. Till now, however, there has not been in modern times any substantial interdisciplinary discussion of power by theology and the social sciences. The absence of such discussion has led either to a mythologizing of power in which ethics seems to vanish, or to an idealistic ethics that ultimately founders on the rocks of power. The question of power is an elusive and perplexing one, about which I dare make only some preliminary comments.

A sort of verbal or ideological "terrorism" has elevated power to the category of a substance, an abstract entity that operates autonomously and is mysteriously held by some, a chimera that one should—or should not—pursue, a monster that devours, or a magic wand that transforms reality. This mythology has been manipulated to instill in people a sense of impotence. It underlies the ideologies of national security. On the other hand, functionalist sociology and political science frequently engage in formal discussions and distinctions which—however necessary in their place—are of little use in the active pursuit of a transformation of society.

For these reasons it would seem that a first task should be to "locate" power in at least four directions. First (though not necessarily first in order of importance), there is the power to affect and control matters of economic decision. The reference here is to the possession or management of the means of production, of financial capital, and of technological know-how in the worldwide trading system. At the same time, there are limits to such power—in the availability of natural resources, the forces of labor, and the "viability" of the existing systems. Second, there is the power to affect and control matters of political decision. The reference here is to the disposition of the mechanisms of the state. More importantly though—as we have seen in our analysis of the failure of military regimes—political power also rests on the ability to obtain a measure of consent, a base of support in society, without which political power disintegrates. Third, there is the power to affect and control an ideological apparatus. Over against purely technocratic or positivistic interpretations of political life, the sociology of knowledge has shown that a society does not exist without some visible or hidden "construction of reality" as a frame of reference. Political power has to rest on that dominant ideology or, short of having to depend exclusively on sheer force, try to have its own ideology "filter through" to the people. Finally, there is the power very precisely to affect or control the disposition of force. This is the ability to use physical strength or coercion to compel obedience and restrain deviancy. It is immaterial whether this force is applied within a framework of law or in some arbitrary way: political power does not exist without a measure of compulsion, without at least the possibility of the use of force. There is no doubt that wherever there is a minimum of consensus, ideological support, and economic viability, modern technology now offers to political power the possibility of maintaining its control through the use of sheer force. But experience tends to show that the limits of such power are extremely narrow.

When these four factors coalesce the result is a consolidated situation in which change becomes almost impossible. But in today's world, where the economic system marginalizes increasing numbers of people and nations, where experience challenges the "constructions of reality" of the dominant classes and peoples, and consensus therefore becomes more and more fragile, the contradictions of power are inevitable. New configurations of power emerge and the correlation of forces changes —circumstantially and locally, to be sure, but the changes add up to a composite picture of situational instability. Thus, while we cannot ignore the phenomenal concentration of power in certain groups, classes, and nations, we should not be mesmerized by the rhetoric of power, as if it were an absolute and monolithic reality.

THE ALL-POWERFUL AND THE POWERLESS

Christian people and churches have had great difficulty dealing with questions of power. Attitudes have oscillated between the poles of absolute rejection and total submission—between the cult of powerlessness and the claims or attempts to exercise absolute power. From the affirmation that all power belongs to God, some have derived a theory of church power. From awareness of the demonic dimension of power, others have been led to a policy of absolute withdrawal. This ambivalence has frequently resulted in a peculiar inability on the part of Christians and churches to participate constructively in political life. A theological ethics of politics must necessarily subject the whole question of power to careful theological discussion. Points to be made in such a discussion would include the following.

(1) Naturally, the Christian faith has always claimed that power belongs to God. Omnipotence has been one of the attributes most consistently and unequivocally assigned to the deity. When we go to the Bible, however, we find that the affirmation of God's power is seldom if ever made in the abstract; it is always related to specific "acts" of God. The classic formula "the great power and the outstretched arm" is used to remind Israel of God's liberating acts, above all the Exodus, and to affirm confidence in God's promised acts of deliverance. Such affirmations are closely related to the idea of the covenant. God discloses his power in faithfulness to the alliance he has established with his people. Even the praise of his power in creation is related to his faithfulness to humankind: his is the power that prevails over the chaos, that sets limits to the onslaught of the forces of destruction and ensures the conditions needed for human life and prosperity.

God's power, therefore, is his active presence—those "powerful acts" of liberation, protection, vengeance, or punishment that correspond to his faithfulness to his people and to the whole of humankind. In other words: God's power is his "justice" in action—in defense of the weak, judgment of the unjust, protection of the powerless, and strengthening of those to whom he has given a mission. It would be difficult to find a better definition of God's power than that of the Magnificat:

> *He has shown strength with his arm,*
> he has scattered the proud in the imagination of their hearts,
> he has put down the mighty from their thrones,
> and exalted those of low degree;
> he has filled the hungry with good things,
> and the rich he has sent empty away.
> He has helped his servant Israel,
> in remembrance of his mercy,
> as he spoke to our fathers,
> to Abraham and to his posterity for ever.
>
> (Luke 1:51–55)

At the same time, two other important features emerge. First, in a world where injustice, oppression, and arrogance are rampant, God's righteous power is affirmed in the midst of conflict. God is engaged in a struggle—his power is manifest in this struggle and is the guarantee of the final triumph of that righteousness of God which is disclosed and presently active in "the mighty acts." Second, such acts are related to human agents—persons, peoples, judges, kings who (whether subjectively aware of it or not) are empowered and commissioned to execute God's righteous judgments of deliverance and of punishment. However miraculously conceived or portrayed, human mediation is the way in which God's power operates in history.

(2) One finds in the Bible both charismatic and institutional "mediations" of political power, judges and kings being clear examples of the distinction. It is therefore particularly interesting to note the ambivalent attitude toward "institutionalized monarchy" represented by the two traditions in 1 Samuel 8—12. The text as we have it (leaving aside the critical questions) suggests two reasons for the institutionalization of the monarchy in Israel: on the one hand the failure of the judges (the sons of Samuel in this case) to "judge," that is, to dispense Jahweh's justice among the people; and on the other hand the people's need to conform to the political model prevalent in their area in order that they might face on equal terms the power of the nations around them. These two conflicting traditions, one accepting monarchy and the other rejecting it, are brought together in the present redaction as a kind of compromise—a more or less grumbling acceptance of the institutionalization of monarchy. This text, however, is not exceptional; it represents a tension in the biblical theology of power which von Rad implies was inevitable and never surmounted.[13]

The text makes its distrust of monarchy explicit in two respects: (a) the institutionalization of kingship represents a rejection of God's direct sovereignty, an attempt to create a human power that will replace the governance of Jahweh; (b) the king will turn the people into servants for himself—his authority will be exploitative and repressive. Again, the text is typical: absolutism and oppression constantly reappear in the Bible as signs of the ambivalence of power. They are among the criteria applied in evaluating the successive kings of Israel and Judah—few if any of whom receive unqualified approval. The model king, on the other hand, usually projected backward to the figure of David and forward to the Anointed One of the messianic kingdom, is esteemed for his lack of absolutism and oppression—for his faithfulness to Jahweh's sovereignty and the exercise of justice.

The human exercise of power, therefore, is caught in this ambivalence: it is a mediation of God's power and justice, but it tends always to absolutize itself and to negate justice. God's power, therefore, is never mediated, as it were, mechanically or automatically through an institution—in this case monarchy. It is mediated rather within the structure of God's justice that corresponds to the covenant. God retains his own authority to judge—and within the conflicts of history to overthrow any power-bearers who overreach themselves and thwart justice.

(3) It is within this framework that we can interpret the much debated question of Jesus' relationship to power. The key to understanding it is found in the logion reported in Mark 10:42–45:

> You know that in the world the recognized rulers lord it over their subjects, and their great men make them feel the weight of their authority. That is not the way with you; among you, whoever wants to be great must be your servant, and whoever wants to be first must be willing to be slave of all. For even the Son of man did not come to be served but to serve, and to surrender his life as a ransom for many. (NEB)

When we read this text in the light of Jesus' temptation, his entry into Jerusalem, and many other texts of the Gospels (including John 10 on the Shepherd) a picture begins to emerge. Jesus is contrasting his own "way of being king" with the rule exemplified by those whose authority the people were at that very time experiencing. The negative features of this picture correspond exactly to those repeatedly singled out for prophetic condemnation—absolutism and oppression. Jesus' mission, on the other hand, is to proclaim and to be the "true king" of prophetic expectation, whose authority is exercised according to God's will, who cares for the poor, who offers himself for his people, who announces and inaugurates "the year of God's liberation." Jesus' rejection of violence is not an isolated characteristic or a new law for politics but the pointed rejection of the most visible and characteristic attitude of the perverted kingship he is denouncing. If this interpretation is correct, then Jesus understood his mission not as one of proposing a model for political action but as one of incarnating in a paradigmatic way God's just and liberating rule, thus setting our understanding of politics on a wholly new course.

(4) The early Christian community saw in the death and resurrection of Jesus the triumph of this messianic kingship over the ambiguous rule of the principalities and powers presently exercising governing authority in this world. These principalities and powers are not done away. Indeed, as they were once instituted, so they still function as "God's

ministers." But in the cross and resurrection of the true King their absolutism and injustice have been successfully challenged and exposed. Insofar as they resist Christ's kingship they are destined to failure and destruction. But they can also serve God's justice and peace. It is for this reason that Christians must pray for them. Thus, political life is neither abolished nor declared outside the ambit of Christ's rule. Rather, the true meaning, judgment, and promise of all ruling has now been disclosed and ensured.

Within the historical conditions of the early church, the concrete exercise of this new understanding of superordination and subordination could be illustrated only within the life of the community. But the scope of this "politics" is universal. Certainty about the "victory of the Lamb" inspires an adamant resistance to all claims of absoluteness on the part of any earthly ruler. The intensity of hope results in a telescoping of time such that the problem of historical mediations disappears.

It is this early Christian understanding that has posed the question for us: How is God's rule of justice—which is paradigmatically disclosed in Jesus Christ and destined to be the true future and the inescapable judgment of all political life—how is it mediated in the struggles of history? We are here thrown back on that "historical identification of priorities" with which we began. But not in a vicious circle, because our "discernment" of priorities has now been informed by and made visible and available in Jesus Christ. Our course must now take us from conviction to strategy.

8

From Conviction to Strategy

In our rough sketch of the path of a theological ethics of politics, we now begin a second movement in the dialectics of praxis and theory. Our attempt here will be to move from the most general and indeterminate to the particular and determinate—from theoretical abstraction to political praxis. This movement is what I have tried to express in the words of the chapter title: "from conviction to strategy." "Strategy," in the military sense in which I use the term, means simply "the art and science of developing and employing" all the resources available for achieving the policy objectives previously defined. Strategy has to be distinguished—even if it cannot be separated—from tactics. In the words of Field Marshal Earl Wavell, "Tactics is the art of handling troops in the battlefield; strategy is the art of bringing forces to the battlefield in a favorable position."[1]

As a way of getting started, I want to go back for a moment to the scenario we used in the historical segment of our road together thus far, namely that of Latin America. To recall our earlier analysis and also as a point of departure for our present concern with strategy, I would present two hypotheses:

(1) We affirm and assume the praxis of Christians who, in the discernment of faith and aware of the historical conditions and challenges of the Latin American situation, have committed themselves to a project of liberation (as characterized in chapter 5).

(2) Given the internal and international conditions, such a project implies a long and painful road and, particularly in some South American countries, a struggle to gain the minimum space and freedom necessary for the people to develop awareness and to create the organizations that can produce change. Thus, while the historical project as such should be clear, there is need in the short term for immediate actions involving alliances and common effort on the basis of fundamental human rights—including social rights—and conditions along the way toward more basic structural change.

The "strategic" question is this: what resources are available in our Christian political understanding and commitment for such a project and prospect? This is not a pragmatic or utilitarian question. We are not interested in "instrumentalizing" Christian faith but in discerning its genuine relevance to the specific ethical questions that emerge in the "praxis of liberation" under existent conditions.

We can organize this preliminary exploration around three questions which are of great importance in this first stage of our return trip to political praxis: (1) How can the people who have introjected oppression over the centuries of domination (including religious domination) be so helped to an awareness of themselves and of their dignity as to conceive a historical project of liberation (and how can the consciousness of those who are blinded by the ideology of domination be unblocked—liberated—for a participation in the struggle of the poor)? Has *the hope of the coming kingdom* any relevance for the birthing amongst an oppressed people of an awareness of liberation in historical terms? (2) Do we have any ethical guidelines—pointers, criteria—to guide our action so far as the possibilities and costs of social change are concerned? Has *the power of the Crucified and Risen Lord* any significance for the crosses and resurrections in the struggle of the people? (3) In the long and painful process, how are personal and communal meaning, integrity, and fulfillment made possible? How can personal life be meaningful when there is no visible success in the historical task to which one is committed? How can the hatred and bitterness of the struggle be transcended so as to retain personal integrity? Has *the love of God* that "has been poured into our hearts through the Holy Spirit" any relevance to keeping intact in the struggle our integrity as human beings?

THE POLITICAL FACE OF THE POOR

Speaking about the political significance of love, Hugo Assmann has raised a fundamental question for a Christian political ethics. "Christians," he says, "still lack a structural model of a living experience of love that has reference to 'the many,' 'the whole of humanity, my neighbor,' and not simply to the particular individual who loves or is loved. Structurally, what is the new dimension of love in the context of a socialized world?"[2] If kingdom-justice and gospel-love meet in the struggle for the liberation of the poor—my neighbor—where are we to find "the political face of the poor"?

In ecumenical discussion today the answer to this question hinges on two categories: class and people. While the former has had more appeal to the "scientific" minds trained in European social thinking, the latter has been crucial in the Third World. Without rejecting the concept of class—or conceding that the two categories are mutually exclusive—I would like to refer briefly to the meaning of the term "people."

Arguing for the centrality of this particular category, the Argentine historian Dussel says:

> Only the category of "people" allows us to understand the process. The people is the "nation" construed as the totality of a political system and a historical culture concretely and geographically given. In its primary signification, mainly and predominantly, "people" means the oppressed working classes. It also means equally the eschatological "outsiders," those excluded ones who, though part of the system . . . are at the same time future and exist as a provocation to justice . . . most typically youth insofar as they are not already dominated by the whole, the system.[3]

If Dussel's characterization of "people" seems imprecise, it nonetheless serves to illustrate the ambiguity of the concept. We cannot escape such ambiguity by simply ignoring the reality to which the term points. Nor can we ignore the fact that, despite—or perhaps on account of—this ambiguity, the concept has played a decisive role in the struggle for liberation at various times and places where the national, cultural, and social dimensions of oppression have been inextricably interwoven.

Interestingly enough, we find the same imprecision and variations in the biblical use of the words for "people." *Laos,* for instance, is used in the Bible to designate simply a collection of people (a crowd without specific identity) as well as to designate a particular people having a specific identity, as in the Septuagint rendering of Gen. 34:22 (rabbinic literature even includes the idea of the particular "genius" of a people). But *laos* is also used for the "common people" as over against the rulers, or upper class. And, obviously, it is also used for "the chosen people," the eschatological congregation of the last days, the people of the covenant.[4] For our purposes the concept becomes crucial in its second and third meanings—a particular historical people and "common people" as distinguished from the ruling class.

Without attempting to specify in detail the relation between class and people, we can say that no analysis of the former can substitute for an analysis of the latter inasmuch as "people" has cultural and ethnic determinations that cannot be reduced to mere epiphenomena of the economic factor. At the same time, "people" cannot be used as a simple collective term for designating everybody without distinction. It is in the interaction between ethnic, cultural, and economic determinations that we can identify the collective reality we call "people." (Indeed, in actual practice this is not terribly difficult—common people are rather keenly aware of who belongs and who does not belong to them.)

As an interesting aside we may note that the Gospels use almost interchangeably "the many" (*hoi polloi*), "the multitude" (*ochlos*), and simply "the people" (*laos*). John 7:45ff. suggests the close interconnection: on the one hand there is "the Sanhedrin and the Pharisees," on the other hand the ignorant multitude (*ochlos*) "who are lost anyway." Here is a clear indication of that schism between the people and the religious—and political—establishment which Metz traces in the contemporary situation.

But there is more yet to be said. Dussel himself has to admit that "if there is an alienated people"—and he has himself indicated that there is—then "'people' is an ambivalent term: it has elements of the best and of the worst connotations." The "people" is a proprietary subject, a bearer in a process of liberation. Otherwise, it is also an "inert mass" that has introjected all the oppression and remains "closed" to any transformation of its existence.[5] It is to this problem that we want now briefly to turn our attention.

THE AWAKENING OF CONSCIOUSNESS

Anthropology and the study of religion have shown that the ethos of a people—its "habitual way of dwelling in the world"—becomes for the persons involved a cosmic fact; the regularity that comprises the customs and mores of a society is assimilated to the regularity of natural phenomena—and thereby placed outside the pale of change. This traditional and sustained character of popular culture is strengthened and sacralized through religious symbols and myths. Severino Croatto in an article on "Popular Culture and Historical Project" has lucidly described the problem: "These values of popular culture imply two consequences: on the one hand, the assimilation to nature gives a circular vision of time; on the other, it fosters a return to the past. What is done today is identified with what was done yesterday; present action must repeat what has always been done and what constitutes a tradition. What then can we do with a popular culture? . . . Is a breakthrough in this mythical consciousness possible without eradicating popular culture?" Croatto himself—along with many Old Testament scholars—points out that such a breakthrough in Weltanschauung did happen in Israel, transposing the existence and action of both God and man from cosmos to history: "As history is privileged over nature, there is an inevitable swing from the cosmogonic and archetypal pole to the teleological and eschatological pole"—and a corresponding increase in the worth and significance of communal praxis and values. What seems to happen at this point is that the cosmic symbols and myths are now reinterpreted and charged with new meaning derived from historical experiences.[6] In the Old Testament this has been clearly shown to have occurred in connection with, among others, the myths of creation and of the flood—reread in the light of the Exodus which has now shaped the collective identity and vocation of the people in history.[7]

Some would claim that such a breakthrough can occur only by way of a process of secularization that destroys the mythological mentality. Facts, however, tend to negate this view, on at least three counts: First, peoples have shown an enormous capacity for remythologizing their relation to the world; this has been true even under the impact of modernization (for instance, in new religious movements, magic, occultism). Second, secularism develops its own ideologies (for instance, "the invisible religion" studied by Max Luckmann), which are equally effective in blocking a teleological vision. Third, and most important, experience has clearly shown that a historical project which is conceived by elites—whether modernizing or socialist—and is "out of touch with the people, far from its implicit aspirations"[8] and unrelated to its culture will be rejected. This has been the experience of many intellectually leftist groups working with Indians and peasants, and even workers. In any case, a liberation obtained "for the people"—but without its participation—by such elites would not be a real liberation.

We must ask, therefore, whether a breakthrough in the mythical consciousness can be reached from within popular culture. The experiences that have inspired "Black Theology" in the United States and "African Theology" and "People's Theology" in Asia represent a positive answer. In his beautiful paper on "Political Theology of Living in Christ with People" C. S. Song revisits an ancient Chinese folk tale about "The Faithful Lady Meng."[9] The story concerns a woman whose husband had been entombed by "the wicked, unjust Emperor Ch'in Shih Huang-ti" during the building of the Great Wall. Song finds here a popular wisdom about oppression and suffering, denunciation and resistance, death and survival that can illumine today's popular struggle vis-à-vis "the cult of national security." "The source of our political theology in Asia is the people," Song writes: "the people humiliated, oppressed, and impoverished."[10] This "People's Theology" is a politics made of tears and endurance, but also of truth and love in the face of greediness, domination, and naked power. Song ends with an expression of faith: "People make history worth experimenting with and worth living. There is no failure in the history created by people. People's history never fails."[11]

With respect to Latin America, it is pertinent to remember that the basic symbols and myths in our popular culture hark back to the introduction of Christianity and the subversion of the Indian ethos by the Spanish colonization. However distorted, modified, or mixed with earlier Indian lore, these symbols and myths carry the biblical story. It is true that, both through such popular adaptation of that story and the use made of these myths and symbols in the subjection of the people, they have been—not only in Latin America—recosmologized and de-historicized. The question now is whether the original explosive power of these symbols and myths—the "dangerous memory" as Metz calls it—can be recovered and reactivated from within the life of the people. Can the "frozen protest" against the world as it is, the story of God's struggle against chaos and injustice to create a human life, the story of the power of the cross and resurrection, be unfrozen and transformed into a historical will for change, into an active hope?

In Latin America this is no longer a question. In the base communities, in the new popular hymnody and singing, and in the struggle for human rights the change has already begun to occur:

In a base community in Central America a peasant hears the words of Jesus: "Come to me, all who labor and are heavy-laden, and I will give you rest" (Matt. 11:28). He responds: "I think Jesus sees above all the suffering of the people. We also carry that burden of exploited people. . . . And I think that Jesus speaks of this burden and that he wants to lighten it."[12]

In the interior of Argentina a congregation brings to the altar a large fish and some tobacco leaves—the fruit of their labors. And they sing Psalm 107: "O, give thanks to the Lord, for he is good. . . . They cried to the Lord in their trouble, and he delivered them from their distress."

In a community in São Paulo a worker comments: "The Pope is right—priests ought not to spend their time on 'material things' like building churches and making collections; they should work at 'spiritual things' like defending and helping the poor."

In a Latin American country a dialogue takes place between a mixed-blood peasant (*mestizo*) being tortured by the police and the officer in charge of the interrogation:

OFFICER: "Where do you get these ideas [about the rights of the poor and the workers]?"

ANSWER: "I got them from my teacher."

OFFICER: "Who is your teacher—name and address?"

ANSWER: "The name is Jesus Christ—the address I don't know, but the teaching you will find in the Gospels."

In the Amazon forests of Brazil a group reenacts the dramatic story of Naboth's vineyard. At the point where Ahab's police force apprehends Naboth, the audience suddenly intervenes spontaneously. It moves in and takes Naboth right out of the hands of the police. "That is not how the story runs in the Bible," comments Clodovis Boff, "but that is how the people lived it in the dramatization. It is the contemporary and creative way in which the people actually read and interpret the Word of God."[13]

Stories such as these could be multiplied thousands of times over. When events of this kind take place, the breakthrough from within the oppressed consciousness has surely begun.

But we must add immediately that such change cannot occur as a purely subjective process. A "conversion" of this sort is always related to historical events and to a historical praxis. It is within the actual struggle of the people—sometimes in minute ways in the little chinks and crannies of the system but sometimes in larger confrontations— that the rebirth of consciousness takes place, where the stories of the faith disclose their "surplus of meaning" and their power to move their hearers. "Conscientization" is this *passah,* or passover—this passage or transition in which, within a historical praxis, the people become aware of the hope and power behind the symbols and stories of their traditional faith and begin to shape a new ethos, a new way of dwelling in the world and in history. It is then that "the people" can indeed become the subject of its own history. This, surely, is a first response—from the point of view of political ethics—to the question of power. But there is, as we said at the beginning of the chapter, a second question.

THE QUEST FOR ETHICAL CRITERIA
FOR ACTION

Do we have any ethical guidelines to guide our action so far as the possibilities and costs of radical social change at a particular juncture in history are concerned? The "discernment" involved in answering this question has a prophetic dimension to it that eludes thoughtful analysis. But it has also a ponderable dimension which is indeed subject to social-ethical scrutiny. Paul Tillich, as we noted already in chapter 3, developed in his early work the concept of *kairos* as a theological-ethical category for political action. Tillich said later in his life: "Europe has missed her providential moment, her *kairos* [the right moment from the point of view of eternity], and tries in vain to escape the destructive consequences of this failure."[14] Was it a real *kairos?* Why was the opportunity thrown away—was it for lack of understanding or lack of commitment?

In Latin America this is by no means a rhetorical or theoretical question. There are those who insist on first ascertaining the presence of all the "objective conditions" needed for social change, on waiting for "the ripe time." But others point out, not without reason, that such objective conditions are never perceived as a result of observation and analysis; usually they are seen only in retrospect—when their absence has frustrated "voluntaristic" efforts, or their presence has rendered fruitful an action undertaken against overwhelming odds.

The history of social change throughout the world—as well as our own history in Latin America—offers instances of both objectivistic procrastination and voluntaristic adventurism. But when the life, the future, the very humanity of millions of people and of generations yet unborn hangs in the balance, such decisions about *kairos* cannot be taken lightly. The "prophetic charism" (not necessarily a religious charism) which "discerns the signs of the times"—in other words the *synthetic* judgment about the consciousness of the people, the conditions for change, and the obstacles—has to be informed by analysis. Elites can easily be mesmerized by their own rhetoric and engage in adventures that leave behind a tragic residue of death and suffering. However, timidity and the spirit of accommodation can easily take refuge behind so-called realism, frequently for purposes of protecting personal advantage or party interest. For this reason I would propose as an instrument of analysis a simple ethical thesis:

> *In carrying out needed structural changes we encounter an inevitable tension between the human cost of their realization and the human cost of their postponement. The basic ethical criterion is the maximizing of universal human possibilities and the minimizing of human costs.*

(1) Here we are speaking not only of the project but also of the process. In the long struggle which we have envisaged, the "human conditions"—that is, the degree of human realization, the improvement of material conditions, and the space for human community—are important both as ends and as means. Therefore in the choice of political tactics it is necessary at each stage to consider carefully the best possibilities for the majority of the people.

(2) The argument about the social cost of structural changes is frequently invoked as a deterrent. Involved here is a not so innocent fallacy: the human cost of postponing such change is not counted. Revolutionary change, it is said, sacrifices human lives. But how many lives are sacrificed by prolonging for a century or two a form of production or distribution of goods that has ceased adequately to serve the needs of the people? "Crash programs," it is said, sacrifice a genera-

tion. But how many generations are sacrificed in the hope of gradual change? Such questions can be multiplied. I am *not* necessarily arguing at this point in favor of revolution or crash programs. I *am* arguing against the verbal terrorism of an ideologically inspired fallacy. Any sound political ethics must be aware of this tension.

(3) As we have seen, the question of power inevitably crops up in any discussion of change. Since social structures once established are recalcitrant about change to any degree, and the power entrenched in the obsolete structures has to be overcome, a countervailing power *for* change must necessarily be built. Historically, this has always meant a mix, variously proportioned, of three constant terms: (a) the pressure for change (from below); (b) consent—or resistance—to change (from the top); and (c) conflict. The human cost of change is determined by the delicate balance of these three terms. Where change rather than order is the basic premise, where justice is the decisive criterion, as we have tried to suggest, then the reduction of human cost—that is, the reduction of conflict—depends on the intensification of the other two terms: pressure for change and consent to change.

We spoke a moment ago about the need for conscientization of the people. But there is also a Christian responsibility for helping the dominant groups break their ideological captivity. This responsibility is particularly important insofar as the churches have access to the dominant sectors of society. The churches need to expose the ideology of oppression and unblock the conscience of Christians so they can participate in a project of liberation. Those who are caught up in the structures of oppression need to hear the call to conversion; they need to hear the good news that the option for the poor is open to them. Here again, it would be possible to recount numerous experiences of the churches—among elites in both the Third World and the central countries. *Although the primary and decisive factor is and must remain the struggle of the oppressed themselves,* this secondary aspect is also significant, not only because it could facilitate change but because the *real* human interests of the oppressive power elites (and of the various middle-sector groups co-opted into their project of oppression) are also at stake. The project of liberation embraces the interests of all because it offers to all better possibilities of human fulfillment. But the ideology of oppression hides this reality from the dominant classes and hardens them in their resistance to change. Hence the importance of the deideologizing task.

(4) Conflict occurs in different forms and with different intensities but

it always involves some measure of violence. I have already discussed elsewhere this question which no political ethics can ignore. Although I will not try here to develop further or even to repeat that discussion,[15] I would like to point out that in any significant consideration of the question of violence, several elements must be taken into account: (a) Violence should not be divorced from the conflict situation in which it is exercised—as if it were an entelechy to be analyzed in itself. This is one of the crucial points in Dom Helder Camara's notion of "the spiral of violence," which is systemic, subversive, and repressive. (b) A distinction must be made between, on the one hand, the "calculated" use of revolutionary violence (which is responsible for the ethical considerations it applies)—even if prompted by spontaneous outbreakings—and the violent "explosions" of peoples long suppressed who have reached the limits of their endurance. (c) The ancient tradition of balancing courage and prudence has here a proper place. The traditional criteria elaborated in discussions about a "just war" still have their relevance. (d) Pacifism—whether in principle or simply of a "practical" kind—has to be considered not in and for itself but only in relation to its incorporation (by means which can claim historical significance) in a project of liberation.

It cannot be sufficiently stressed that we have been dealing here with some *theoretical* ethical criteria which have been abstracted from real political praxis and stated in general terms. Most frequently, these issues are decided in a dialectic between the people and its leaders (the groups that have sometimes been called condensers of the popular consciousness), a dialectic that takes place in the midst of the struggle. Questions arise and are usually solved at the level of tactics. Political praxis hardly lends itself to the kind of abstractions we have been using. Only a living relation between the leaders and the people, only the "sense" of what is right at any given moment can prevail. But we are not thereby relieved of all responsibility for theoretical work—which precisely in critical situations enters, whether consciously or not, into the shaping of concrete decisions. We are dealing here not with universal norms but with tentative ethical formulations that are offered as resources in the struggle.

Perhaps I may be permitted to place this question of theoretical analysis back into theological context by speaking of it as a question of "discernment." Human participation in the dynamics of the theological enterprise is not the product of some intellectual operation or equation. It is a risk undertaken in the encounter of love, sensitivity, and knowl-

edge, and—in the case of our Christian faith—is finally vindicated only
on "that day." As Paul puts it in Phil. 1:9–11, au. trans.:

> . . . that your *love* may abound more and more in knowledge [*epignōsis*—
> the intelligent knowledge of God's purpose, of his *oikonomia*] and percep-
> tion [*aisthēsis*—the practical discernment of his will] . . . that you may be
> able to judge [*dokimazein*—prove that which has value] between alterna-
> tives [*ta diapheronta*] . . . so that you may be found rich in the harvest of
> justice (in the day of Christ), to the glory and praise of God.

Epilogue:
Love Incarnate

Our quotation from Hugo Assmann on the "social reference of love," given early in the preceding chapter, continues in this way:

> With respect to the rich experience in which the personal need to love and to be loved is realized, what is the meaning of giving one's life for one's brother within the wider context of the historical process? Is there not a need here to enlarge the parameters of our experiential references in our understanding of the gratuitousness of love?[1]

When we speak about a project of liberation, we are talking about persons—about irreplaceable human subjects, unique human faces. We see such persons, however, not in the isolation of individualism, not as "private possessors," nor yet as amalgamated into a mass reduced to occasional bearers of natural and social determinations. When we speak about liberation we are also talking about a long struggle, and therefore about suffering and death—the suffering and deprivation and misery, the suffering of the innocent caught in the midst of the struggle, the suffering of those who will invest their lives in a project of liberation but will die "this side of the Jordan." But we are also talking about the suffering of the oppressors, about their anxiety, their fear of being dispossessed (which in their ideological blindness they count as death because they have defined the whole meaning of their lives by their possessions) and in some cases of being physically eliminated. An authentic political ethics cannot avoid these questions because they are central to a real political life that is compatible with the term "liberation."

Involved here is a whole cluster of issues—personal identity, personal meaning in life, suffering, death, transcendence—that a political ethics must explore. Here is where the fundamental motif of love finds its locus in political ethics. In the Scriptures, in fact, love is not a general category explained in isolation; love is God's "mode of action," the ontological life style (if such a contradiction in terms is admissible) of God in *his*

111

project of creation and redemption—to which the human "partner" is both invited and empowered. It is in the sphere of historical commitment, under the eschatological promise, that love finds its proper context. Assmann, who can hardly be suspect of falling prey to bourgeois subjectivism, offers this conclusion following a devastating critique of the ideological use of Christian love:

> Every attempt to discover a human motivation for the struggle for liberation sooner or later comes up against the need to inquire into the meaning of the radical praxis of dying for others. We know that many die for their brethren, and others incorporate such death into their life-project as something accepted beforehand—against the time when it will actually occur—without feeling the need to "theologize" their option. But that which is realized in this option implies an even more radical question if such option is to be humanly assumed, that is, assumed with an awareness of its historical meaning. This radical question is theological.[2]

It is important to notice the importance that this radical motivation of love and the motif of "laying down one's life" for the brothers and sisters has played and continues to play in liberation language in Latin America. It is central in the thought of even the more radical leaders. Perhaps it is a testimony to the Christian presence within such movements; perhaps it is the age-old Christian tradition asserting itself—in a diffused way—even among non-Christians. In any case, this love-language stands in sharp contrast to the hate-language of repression with its constant mythologizing of the struggle and "demonizing" of the enemy. In the mind and conscience of the Latin Americans committed to liberation, we are engaged in a project of love, not of hatred. I would like to suggest now some tracks along which this insight could be pursued as a resource for ethical reflection.

The first track has to do with the matter of personal identity, the reality of the human subject engaged in the project. A "militant's identity" cannot be established in isolation, as some kind of a monad related to some absolutely transcendent ground or cause of existence, nor can it be established in separation from the project to which he or she is committed. In any struggle there is always the temptation to establish one's identity in relation to the enemy—the other regarded as "threat" (there is a whole philosophical elaboration of this theme). In the peoples' movements, in the base communities, there is a contrary movement—to find one's identity, the ground of one's subjecthood, in one's brother, with whom and for whom I live, struggle, and am ready to lay down my life. This "other" is perceived, not as denying me but as affirming me. In the Christian community—to which many of these people are related—grace and love thus flow into one another: I affirm God in my brothers and sisters, and I affirm them in God.

But a second dimension enters the picture—the fact of hatred. It would be less than honest to deny the hatred that is generated in any struggle. "Your virtue," says Nietzsche correctly, "is worth nothing if it cannot become indignant." Love does not dissolve the reality of the enemy; it relativizes it. There is an element of Manichaeism in any struggle: the more the struggle escalates in quantity and quality and the longer it is prolonged, the stronger the hatred becomes. I will not soon forget the strange plea of a Jewish mother whose son had "disap-peared" in a wave of repression: "Pastor, for God's sake, help me; I feel that I have begun to hate!" The dialectic of love for the brother and hatred for the enemy will always be present. But which is a "function" of the other?—that is the important question. If hatred of the enemy is subordinated to love for the brother and sister, then the struggle is made "functional," and the possibility of affirming the humanity of the enemy during and after the struggle remains open. This is the kind of ethics of liberation which many—Christians and non-Christians—are trying to develop within the project of liberation.

Third, there is the question of transcendence, which our European and American friends and colleagues keep raising. Does not a project of liberation conceived from an eschatological perspective—related posi-tively to God's kingdom—run the risk of idolatry, of absolutization? At this point they appeal to "the eschatological reservation." Without entering into a full discussion of the question in this limited space, I would suggest that the problem of transcendence should really be discussed in connection with love, where both eschatology and history, both God's kingdom and human society, find their meaning, goal, distance, and unity.

With this new direction in mind Paul Lehmann has taken a creative fresh look at Karl Barth's old commentary on Romans 13, which has haunted many politically inclined disciples of Barth, myself included. In it Barth says: "Love is man's existential standing before God, man's being touched by the freedom of God and in this confrontation being established as a person. . . . The protest against the course of this world should be *made* through 'mutual love' and not be abandoned." To which Lehmann comments: "Love exalts the humanity of the neighbor above the cause that proclaims its advent, and transfigures the passion of revolution so that its promise may in truth be born. Love frees the revolution for the practice of truth in its cause."[3]

A project of liberation is freed from the danger of absolutization not by being relativized from the outside by some extrinsic principle or perspective—which in the final analysis always becomes reactionary—but by being related to its own inner meaning, which is love. Love is thus the inner meaning of politics, just as politics is the outward form of love. When this relation is made operative in the struggle for liberation, there is both the flexibility necessary for humanizing the struggle and the freedom necessary for humanizing the result of the struggle.

Finally, as a fourth track, there is the question of death. "As long as there is suffering and death," a communist friend once told me, "faith will be necessary." (We have already seen in chapter 7 that Ernst Bloch had the courage to face this issue.) We might think to explain an affirmation of this kind in a variety of ways (though always with caution, as Bonhoeffer has taught us!). But the experience is there. Any pastor or priest or social worker—indeed any committed person—connected with the protracted proceedings that end in death needs no further explanation. Johannes Metz quotes a letter of the German Catholic bishops which—whatever may have been its purpose and intent—puts the question forcefully:

> It is deeply inhuman to forget or to suppress this question of the life of the dead, because it implies a forgetfulness and a suppression of past [and present] suffering and an acceptance of the meaninglessness of that suffering. Finally, the happiness of the descendants cannot compensate for the suffering of the ancestors and social progress cannot make up for the injustice done to the dead. If we accept for too long that death is meaningless and are indifferent towards the dead, we shall in the end only be able to offer trivial promises to the living.[4]

Hugo Assmann's suggestion now becomes relevant that we need to take up again the theology of the Cross, the "remembrance of the passion, death, and resurrection of Jesus Christ." It is not enough simply to recover the context of his death in a situation of political conflict, and hence its character as political event (though this too is indispensable). As Moltmann and Sobrino have emphasized, there is beyond that another decisive question—God's silence in face of the cross of Jesus. When in his struggle on behalf of the kingdom and against the structures of injustice and idolatry Jesus is condemned and executed, the Father—whose presence and power had been attested in Jesus' ministry—"absents himself." Like so many others who have suffered defeat in the course of human history, Jesus dies "abandoned by God." If God is present in the death of Christ—and on this the whole

Christian faith stands or falls—he is not present as transcendent Power overruling human injustice and oppression from the outside, but as Jesus' own power of truth and love operating "from within" to surrender his life "for the many."

Precisely here, in this "gap" of God's presence, faith finds its own possibility and praxis. The resurrection comes not to cancel out the cross, not to ensure a visible victory, but rather to confirm Jesus' praxis of love and justice and thus to invite a participation in that praxis, in the sure hope that such praxis is not lost but always recovered and incorporated in the future of the kingdom. The power of death is not magically suspended, but the praxis of vicarious love ("laying down our life for the brethren") through death reaches its final consummation. This is not merely an assertion about the triumph of a cause, but the confession of a faith in the historical and eternal vindication of innocent suffering and committed love (and of those who personally bear them). Confident following is the correlate of the Cross.

Notes

1
THE NEED
FOR A POLITICAL ETHICS

1. Aristotle, *Ethica Nichomachea,* Book I, ch. 2, trans. W. D. Ross in *The Basic Works of Aristotle,* ed. Richard McKeon (New York: Random House, 1941), 1094 ab., pp. 935–36. Italics added.

2. Edward A. Ross, *Sin and Society* (Boston and New York: Houghton Mifflin, 1907), p. 31.

3. From an anonymous paper (see p. 1).

4. *The International Herald Tribune,* 22 October 1980, p. 6, European edition.

5. Helmut Schelsky, quoted in Jürgen Habermas, *Towards a Rational Society: Student Protest, Science, and Politics,* trans. Jeremy Shapiro (Boston: Beacon Press, 1970), p. 59.

6. See Marcos Arruda, ed., *Transnational Corporations, Technology, and Human Development* (Geneva: World Council of Churches/Commission on the Churches' Participation in Development, 1980).

7. Admiral Hyman B. Rickover, "Address to the Joint Economic Committee of Congress"; Jan. 28, 1982.

8. Friedrich A. von Hayek, "Individualism: True and False," in *Individualism and Economic Order* (Chicago: University of Chicago Press, 1948), p. 32. Italics added.

9. Franz Hinkelammert, "The Mystique of Transnational Business and the Vision of a Just Society" (Geneva: World Council of Churches, 1981, Mimeographed).

10. Habermas, *Towards a Rational Society,* p. 60.

11. Robert L. Heilbroner, *An Inquiry Into the Human Prospect* (New York: W. W. Norton & Co., 1974), p. 22.

12. Ibid., p. 136.

13. Ibid., pp. 136f.

14. See John C. Bennett, *The Radical Imperative: From Theology to Social Ethics* (Philadelphia: Westminster Press, 1975).

15. Niccolò Machiavelli, *The Prince,* quoted in *Machiavelli, Cynic, Patriot*

or Political Scientist, ed. De Lamar Jensen (Lexington, Mass.: D. C. Heath Co., 1960), p. 13.

16. Benedetto Croce, *Politics and Morals,* trans. Salvatore J. Castiglione (New York: Philosophical Library, 1945), p. 59.

17. Max Lerner, "Introduction" in *The Prince and the Discourses of Machiavelli* (New York: Random House, 1950).

18. Thomas Hobbes, *Leviathan,* ch. 17.

19. Gérard Lebrun, *O que é poder* (São Paulo: Editora Brasiliense, 1981), p. 33.

2
CHRISTIAN RESPONSES
TO THE ETHICAL DILEMMA

1. Ernst Troeltsch, *Christian Thought: Its History and Application* (New York: World Publishing, Meridian Books, 1952), p. 179.

2. *Luther's Works,* vol. 35, ed. Jaroslav Pelikan and Helmut T. Lehmann (Philadelphia: Fortress Press, 1960), pp. 81–129.

3. For a comparison between Luther and Augustine on this question see Heinrich Bornkamm, *Luther's Doctrine of the Two Kingdoms* (Philadelphia: Fortress Press, 1966), pp. 19–28, on whose excellent and concise presentation I have relied at several points in this section.

4. In a little book published in 1933 under the significant title *Die deutsche Stunde der Kirche* (Göttingen: Vandenhoeck & Ruprecht, 1933) Paul Althaus builds on a supposed revelation of God present in history (and specifically in the *Volk*) to support the position of those who "greeted the German transformation of 1933 as a gift and miracle of God" (p. 5). Althaus exhorts the ministers of the church to regard "pastoral care" of "the whole soul of the people"—that is, recovery of the German identity—as "the church's objective" (p. 60). Although he tries to raise defenses against a paganization of the gospel, his booklet shocks by the way it gives religious sanction to "German nationalism" without at the same time trying to bring the contents of the gospel to bear on the nature and purpose of that nationalism. The unity and the separation of the two kingdoms thus work together to produce an acceptance of the new ideology without any effort to transform it.

5. Karl Barth, "First Letter to the French Protestants," English translation in Karl Barth, *A Letter to Great Britain from Switzerland* (London: Sheldon Press, 1941), pp. 36f. Barth nevertheless adds: "Every people has just such a heritage from paganism and from certain Christian errors which have strengthened this paganism."

6. Gustaf Wingren, *Luther on Vocation* (Philadelphia: Fortress Press, 1957).

7. Ibid., p. 30.

8. Martin Luther, quoted by Bornkamm, *Luther's Doctrine,* p. 7.

9. In this case, when the prince asked the people in Luther's community to

turn over their New Testaments to be destroyed, such an instance is exemplified.

10. Adolf von Harnack, "The Evangelical Social Mission in the Light of the History of the Church" in Adolf von Harnack and Wilhelm Herrmann, *Essays on the Social Gospel* (New York: G. P. Putnam's Sons, 1907), pp. 82–84. Italics added. The original paper was first read May 17, 1894 at the Evangelical Social Congress.

11. Ibid.

12. Ibid.

13. Karl Marx, "On James Mill," in *Early Texts* ed. and trans. D. McLellan (New York: Barnes & Noble, 1971), p. 192.

14. Karl Marx, "The Communism of the 'Rheinischer Beobachter,'" vol. 4 of Karl Marx and Friedrich Engels, *Werke* (Berlin: Dietz Verlag, 1959–71), p. 200.

15. Marx, "On the Jewish Question," *Early Texts*, p. 99.

16. For good presentations of the social thinking of the World Council of Churches, see Edward Duff, S.J., *The Social Thought of the World Council of Churches* (New York: Association Press, 1956); Carl-Henric Grenholm, *Christian Social Ethics in a Revolutionary Age* (Uppsala: Verbum, 1973); and Paul Bock, *The Search for a Responsible World Society* (Philadelphia: Westminster Press, 1974).

17. Richard Shaull, "Revolutionary Change in Theological Perspective," in *Christian Social Ethics in a Changing World: An Ecumenical Theological Inquiry* ed. John Coleman Bennett (New York: Association Press, 1966), p. 36.

18. Ibid.

19. *World Conference of Church and Society: Official Report* (Geneva: World Council of Churches, 1966), p. 202.

20. "Continuing an Old Discussion in a New Context" (Geneva: World Council of Churches/Commission on the Churches' Participation in Development, October 1980, Mimeographed).

21. Unfortunately I have been unable to make extensive use of the valuable materials produced by the consultation on "political ethics" sponsored by the World Council of Churches/Commission on the Churches' Participation in Development at Cyprus, October 18–25, 1981.

22. Josef Höffner, *Manual de doctrina social Cristiana* (Madrid: Ediciones Rialp, 1974), p. 14; cf. the ET by Geoffrey Stevens, *Fundamentals of Christian Sociology* (Westminster, Md.: Newman Press, 1965), p. 14.

23. John Howard Yoder, *The Politics of Jesus: Vicit Agnus Noster* (Grand Rapids: Wm. B. Eerdmans, 1972).

24. John Howard Yoder, ed., *Textos Escogidos de la Reforma Radical* (Buenos Aires: Editorial La Aurora, 1976), p. 15.

25. Yoder, *Politics of Jesus*, pp. 62f.

26. Ibid., p. 98.

27. Ibid., p. 157.

28. See below pp. 47–49 and 79ff.

3
FROM PRAXIS
TO THEORY AND BACK

1. Ernst Troeltsch, *The Social Teaching of the Christian Churches,* vol. 1 (New York: Macmillan Co., 1931), p. 33.
2. Ibid., pp. 30f.
3. In this chapter, and particularly in its first two sections, I shall borrow heavily from what I consider to be the best systematic discussion of method-ological questions related to a theology of politics, namely that of Clodovis Boff, O.S.M., *Teologia e Pratica: Teologia do Politico e suas Mediações* (Petrópolis, Brazil: Vozes Editôra Ltda., 1978). I shall refer particularly to his Section III, in some cases summarizing Boff's arguments, though naturally the interpretation and use of these ideas is my own.
4. Boff, *Teologia,* p. 368.
5. Maximilien Rubel, *Páginas Escogidas de Marx para una Ética Socialista,* vol. 1 (Buenos Aires: Amorrortu Editores, 1974), pp. 11ff.
6. Quoted by Marx in the "Postface" to the second edition of *Das Kapital.*
7. Karl Marx and Friedrich Engels, *Selected Correspondence: 1846–1895,* trans. Dona Torr (New York: International Publications, 1942), p. 219.
8. Sidney Hook, *Towards an Understanding of Karl Marx: A Revolutionary Interpretation* (New York: John Day, 1933), p. 113. Italics added.
9. For the early development and articulation of the *kairos* idea in Paul Tillich, in the "Kairos Circle" and articles between 1920 and 1926, see the work of my colleague John R. Stumme, *Socialism in Theological Perspective: A Study of Paul Tillich 1918–1933* (Missoula, Mont.: Scholars Press, 1978).
10. See José Míguez Bonino, *Christians and Marxists* (Grand Rapids: Wm. B. Eerdmans, 1976), pp. 94–102.
11. See below pp. 84ff.
12. See among others the sharp analysis and critique of Franz Hinkel-ammert, *Las Armas Ideológicas de la Muerte* (Costa Rica: Educa, 1977), pp. 125–50.
13. See Boff, *Teologia,* p. 76.
14. See Gaston Bachelard, *Le Rationalisme Appliqué* (Paris: Presses Univer-sitaires de France, 1970), chap. 6; idem, *Le Materialisme Rationnel* (Paris: Presses Universitaires de France, 1963), pp. 207ff.
15. See Robert K. Merton, *The Sociology of Science* (Chicago: University of Chicago Press, 1973), pp. 173–253.
16. We must be aware, naturally, that these are very broad and imprecise characterizations of whole "families" of sociological approaches rather than two neatly distinct sociological doctrines. Moreover, there is a mutual interpen-etration of the two approaches. Nevertheless I think we are justified in stressing the basic difference between these two perspectives on society. For a discerning and thought-provoking discussion of the relation between theology and sociol-

ogy see Gregory Baum, *Religion and Alienation: A Theological Reading of Sociology* (New York: Paulist Press, 1975).

17. In this sense it is instructive to follow Talcott Parsons in his discussion of class conflict, which, through analysis, he finally reduces to a sort of circumstantial maladjustment. See his "Social Classes and Class Conflict in the Light of Recent Sociological Theory," in Talcott Parsons, *Essays in Sociological Theory,* rev. ed. (New York: Free Press, 1954), pp. 323–35.

18. See Boff, *Teologia,* pp. 370–73, the diagram being on p. 371.

19. Boff distinguishes between theology A, which directly addresses specific theological subjects such as God, grace, and sin; and theology B, which "theologizes" common human concerns such as sex, politics, and aesthetics. Such a distinction of course cannot be drawn too sharply, since in fact both theologies are always present, whether explicitly or implicitly, at any given time. Nonetheless, some such distinction of "intention" is necessary for hermeneutical and methodological reasons. It should therefore be clear that, while throughout this book we are dealing with theology B, this in no way minimizes the need or importance of the classical theological "loci."

20. See Paul Ricoeur, "Universal Civilization and National Cultures" in *History and Truth,* trans. Charles A. Kelbley (Evanston, Ill.: Northwestern University Press, 1965), pp. 271–84; and Enrique Dussel, *A History of the Church in Latin America: Colonialism to Liberation (1492–1979),* trans. Alan Neely (Grand Rapids; Wm. B. Eerdmans, 1981), pp. 21–26.

21. Nicos Poulantzas, *Clases sociales y poder político en el estado capitalista* (México: Siglo Veintiuno, 1969), p. 15; his "Introduccion" deals in depth with social formation.

22. The concept of historical block is explained in the political writings of Antonio Gramsci. See specifically his *Note sul Machiavelli, sulla politica e sullo stato moderno* (Torino: Giulio Einaudi, 1949), especially the section on "Analise delle situazione."

23. I owe this definition to a course on sociology taught by Professor Christian Lalive d'Epinay at the Instituto Superior Evangélico de Estudios Teológicos in Buenos Aires in 1969.

24. Hugo Assmann, *Teología desde la Praxis de la Liberación: Ensayo Teológico desde la América Dependiente* (Salamanca, Spain: Ediciones Sígueme, 1973), p. 159. The English translation by Paul Burns, *Theology for a Nomad Church* (Maryknoll, N.Y.: Orbis Books, 1976), is incomplete.

4
LATIN AMERICA:
FROM AUTHORITARIANISM TO
DEMOCRACY

1. Paul Lehmann, *The Transfiguration of Politics* (New York: Harper & Row, 1975), p. 155.

2. Orlando Fals-Borda, *Subversion and Social Change in Colombia* (New York: Columbia University Press, 1969), p. 3.

3. Hubert Herring, *A History of Latin America* (New York: Alfred A. Knopf, 1967), p. 78.

4. Ibid.

5. Enrique Dussel, *A History of the Church in Latin America: Colonialism to Liberation (1492–1979)*, trans. Alan Neely (Grand Rapids: Wm. B. Eerdmans, 1981), p. 38.

6. Fals-Borda, *Subversion,* p. 40.

7. For an expanded treatment of the nature of colonial society, as well as for further historical analysis, see Tulio Halperin Donghi, *Historia Contemporánea de América Latina,* 5th ed. (Madrid: Alianza Editorial, 1975); abridged English translation by Josephine de Bunsen in *The Aftermath of the Revolution in Latin America* (New York: Harper & Row, 1973).

8. Fals-Borda, *Subversion,* p. 48.

9. See the essay by Georges Casalis, "Jesús, ni vencido ni monarca celestial" in *Jesús, ni Vencido ni Monarca Celestial,* ed. José Míguez Bonino (Buenos Aires: Tierra Nueva, 1978). English translation in preparation by Orbis Books.

10. Henri Desroche, "Sociologie religieuse et sociologie fonctionelle," in *Archives de Sociologie des Religions* 23 (January–June 1967): 10–17.

11. See also Joachim Wach, *Sociology of Religion* (Chicago: University of Chicago Press, 1944), pp. 162, 173.

12. For a fuller discussion of this question and a bibliography on it, see Dussel, *A History;* see also Hans Jürgen Prien, *Die Geschichte des Christentums in Lateinamerika* (Göttingen: Vandenhoeck & Ruprecht, 1978), paragraphs 23–25.

13. Dussel, *A History,* p. 94.

14. W. Stanley Rycroft, *Religion and Faith in Latin America* (Philadelphia: Westminster Press, 1958), esp. chaps. 6–8.

15. Samuel Guy Inman, *Ventures in Inter-American Friendship* (New York: Missionary Education Movement of the United States and Canada, 1975), pp. 6–7.

16. Quoted in Robert E. Speer, *The Unfinished Task of Foreign Missions* (London and Edinburgh: Fleming H. Revell, Co., 1926), pp. 219–20.

5
LATIN AMERICA:
FROM DEMOCRACY TO THE
NATIONAL SECURITY STATE

1. This excellent summary of the APRA program is given by José Comblin in *The Church and the National Security State* (Maryknoll, N.Y.: Orbis Books, 1979), p. 58.

2. Ibid.

3. There is an interesting discussion of this topic as it relates to Latin America in Julio Barreiro, *Los Molinos de la Ira* (México: Siglo Veintiuno, 1980).

4. Comblin, *Church and National Security State*, p. 57.

5. The basic elements of this doctrine of national security were elaborated, as regards Latin America, in the military circles of the U.S. After the success of the Cuban revolution, which radicalized the options of the Latin American left, the U.S. formulated and put into operation its programs of military assistance. Samuel P. Huntington's doctrines (see *The Soldier and the State: The Theory and Politics of Civil Military Relations* [Cambridge, Mass.: Harvard University Press, 1957]) began to gain popularity in Latin American military circles. This was the genesis of that "military subversion" of political life which the armies undertook in many Latin American countries, particularly in the southern cone. See Noam Chomsky and Edward S. Herman, *The Washington Connection and Third World Fascism* (Boston: South End Press, 1979); and Holly Sklar, ed., *Trilateralism: The Trilateral Commission and Elite Planning for World Management* (Boston: South End Press, 1980).

6. Comblin, *Church and National Security State*, p. 68.

7. *Cuartelazos* (from *cuartel* meaning barracks) are purely personal, or factional, military coups, usually little more than a changing of the guard, without deep political or social implications.

8. The Commission Report is published in the *Revista de la Comisión Internacional de Juristas* 17 (Dec. 12, 1976).

9. See Hugo Assmann, *Teología desde la Praxis de la Liberación: Ensayo Teológico desde la América Dependiente* (Salamanca, Spain: Ediciones Sígueme, 1973), pp. 216ff.

10. Orlando Fals-Borda, *Subversion and Social Change in Colombia* (New York: Columbia University Press, 1969), pp. 63–65.

11. The collapse of the military regime in Argentina, precipitated by the South Atlantic conflict but already anticipated by mounting popular protests, by the loudly decried economic collapse, and by the signs of internal conflict and disintegration within the armed forces, is a clear example and proof of our thesis. The Argentine experience parallels the chaotic situation in Bolivia, the desperate attempts of the Uruguayan government (after a "plebiscite" to legitimize their plans had provoked, despite strong pressure, a massive rejection) to stay in power by offering expanded participation to political forces, and the recognition by the Chilean government of the failure of its economic policy.

12. Gustavo Gutiérrez, *A Theology of Liberation: History, Politics, and Salvation*, trans. Caridad Inda and John Eagleson (Maryknoll, N.Y.: Orbis Books, 1973), p. 237.

6
JUSTICE AND ORDER

1. William Temple, *Nature, Man, and God* (New York: Macmillan Co., 1949), p. 478.

2. Karl Barth, *The Humanity of God* (Richmond: John Knox Press, 1960), p. 51.

3. Temple, *Nature,* p. 478.

4. Dietrich Bonhoeffer, *Ethics,* ed. Eberhard Bethge, trans. Neville Horton Smith (New York: Macmillan Co., 1955), p. 22.

5. Protestantism is sometimes prone to a christological reductionism in which creation and the dynamism of history are almost deprived of all theological meaning. In Catholic natural theology, on the other hand, the autonomy of creation as perceived by reason becomes a foundation for apologetics and ethics in which the specificity of the Christian revelation is almost lost to sight. A fully trinitarian approach, by contrast, not only strengthens the positive aspect of the "two kingdoms" idea—God's "distinct" presence as Father and Son—but also precludes the danger which has beset it, namely an emancipation of the secular kingdom from the influence of the gospel.

6. Paul Lehmann, *The Transfiguration of Politics* (New York: Harper & Row, 1975), p. 230. Italics added.

7. Ibid.

8. Ibid.

9. Ibid., pp. 231–32.

10. Augustine *City of God* 4.4.

11. See Augustine *Letter to Macedonius* 153.26.

12. See Augustine *Letter to the Rogatist Bishop Vincent* 93.50.

13. See Augustine *Letter to Macedonius* 153.26.

14. Lehmann, *Transfiguration of Politics,* p. 77.

15. So much biblical scholarship has been devoted to these themes over the last two decades that it is hardly necessary to argue the point in detail. Although there are still many controverted issues, the basic framework of interpretation can be regarded as a matter of accepted consensus in biblical interpretation.

16. Gerhard von Rad, *Old Testament Theology,* vol. 1 of *The Theology of Israel's Historical Traditions,* trans. D. M. G. Stalker (New York: Harper & Row, 1962), p. 370.

17. There is, therefore, no qualitative change in the Pauline concept of the "justification of the sinner," except when some, by interpreting it in purely juridical terms derived from Roman law rather than from the Old Testament, attempt to establish a basic dichotomy between God's "justice" in justification and the performance of justice demanded from the human being. In practice if not in theory this tragic misunderstanding of righteousness-justice has been the ideological instrument for divorcing faith and love, dogmatics and ethics, God's grace and man's responsibility.

18. Jürgen Moltmann has given a succinct and excellent summation of this point in *The Crucified God: The Cross of Christ as the Foundation and Criticism of Christian Theology,* trans. R. A. Wilson and John Bowden (New York: Harper & Row, 1974), pp. 136–45.

19. Karl Barth, *Church Dogmatics* II/2, ed. G. W. Bromiley (Edinburgh: T. & T. Clark, 1957), p. 513.

7
HOPE AND POWER

1. See Herbert W. Richardson, "What Makes a Society Political?" in *Religion and Political Society,* ed. Jürgen Moltmann et al. (New York: Harper & Row, 1974), pp. 100–120, esp. pp. 100–101, 114–19.

2. Herbert W. Richardson, *Toward an American Theology* (New York: Harper & Row, 1967), p. 16.

3. Ibid., p. 29.

4. This is the significance of John C. Bennett's book, *The Radical Imperative: From Theology to Social Ethics* (Philadelphia: Westminster Press, 1975). Without disavowing his previous works, Bennett recognizes the radically new situation—for which "realism" is not enough.

5. Thomas G. Sanders, *Christianity and Crisis,* 33/15 (Sept. 17, 1973).

6. Ibid., p. 170.

7. Ibid., p. 173. Italics added.

8. Ibid., p. 175.

9. Pope Paul VI, *Octogesima Adveniens,* par. 37 (May 15, 1971).

10. Leonardo Boff, *Jesus Christ Liberator: A Critical Christology for Our Times* (Maryknoll, N.Y.: Orbis Books, 1978), pp. 134–38, 280–82.

11. Pope Paul VI, *Octogesima Adveniens,* par. 37 (May 15, 1971).

12. There is in Gutiérrez a certain imprecision. While he speaks of the utopia of "a new man and a new society," he continues to identify it at several points with a more precise historical project along the lines we have indicated in chapter 5. I think it is better to maintain a distinction between the guiding "vision," represented by the utopia, and a more concrete historical project.

13. Gerhard von Rad, *Old Testament Theology,* vol. 1 of *The Theology of Israel's Historical Traditions* (New York: Harper & Row, 1962), pp. 39ff.

8
FROM CONVICTION TO STRATEGY

1. *The Encyclopedia Americana* 25:772, s.v. "strategy" by Vincent J. Esposito.

2. Hugo Assmann, *Teología desde la Praxis de la Liberación: Ensayo Teológico desde la América Dependiente* (Salamanca, Spain: Ediciones Sígueme, 1973), p. 69.

3. Enrique Dussel, *Método para una Filosofía de la Liberación* (Salamanca, Spain: Ediciones Sígueme, 1974), p. 226.

4. See Gerhard Kittel, ed., *Theological Dictionary of the New Testament,* trans. Geoffrey W. Bromiley (Grand Rapids: Wm. B. Eerdmans, 1967), s.v. *"laos,"* vol. IV, pp. 29–57.

5. Enrique Dussel, *Teología de la liberación e historia,* vol. 1 (Caminos de Liberación Latinoamericana. Buenos Aires: edición del autor, 1975), p. 159.

6. See Severino Croatto, "Cultura popular y proyecto histórico," in *Cuadernos Salmantinos de Filosofía* 3 (1977): 371–74.

7. If George Mendenhall's thesis is correct that certain poor groups, marginal to the Palestinian kingdoms, groups which did not participate in the Exodus, nonetheless joined the covenant and accepted the exodus tradition as their own, we would have an even more impressive instance of the kind of transformation of consciousness of which we are speaking.

8. Croatto, "Cultura popular," p. 372.

9. See C. S. Song, *The Tears of Lady Meng: A Parable of People's Political Theology* (Geneva: World Council of Churches, 1981), which includes not only the brief folk tale but the entire lecture given at the General Assembly of the Christian Conference of Asia held in Bangalore, India, May 18–28, 1981. Song's moving paper is puzzling in its rejection of any discussion of political means. Nonetheless, it is a profound interpretation of the powers of denunciation and of truth, and of the significance of the "power of tears" of the people—which those of us coming from a Western tradition should try carefully to understand before taking issue with it. It would be interesting to compare Song's interpretation of ancient lore with Mao's use of many of the same folk stories.

10. Ibid., p. 43.

11. Ibid., p. 65.

12. See Ernesto Cardenal, *The Gospel in Solentiname* (Maryknoll, N.Y.: Orbis Books, 1978), vol. 2, p. 14.

13. Clodovis Boff, *Deus e o Homem no Inferno Verde: Quatro Meses de Convivência com as CEBs do Acre* (Petrópolis, Brazil: Vozes Editôra Ltda., 1980), p. 83.

14. Paul Tillich, "An Historical Diagnosis: Impressions of a European," *Radical Religion* 2/1 (Winter 1936): 11.

15. See José Míguez Bonino, "Violence and Liberation," *Christianity and Crisis* 32/12 (July 10, 1972): 169–72.

EPILOGUE:
LOVE INCARNATE

1. Hugo Assmann, *Teología desde la praxis de la liberación: Ensayo teológico desde la América dependiente* (Salmanca, Spain: Ediciones Sígueme, 1973), p. 69.

2. Ibid., p. 76.

3. Paul Lehmann, *The Transfiguration of Politics* (New York: Harper & Row, 1975), p. 47. The Barth quotation is Lehmann's translation of a segment from Barth's *Römerbrief*, 5th ed., 1929, p. 477.

4. Johannes B. Metz, *Faith in History and Society: Toward a Practical Fundamental Theology* (New York: Seabury Press, 1980), p. 75.